Also by JULIANA BUHRING

NOT WITHOUT MY SISTER

THIS ROAD I RIDE

SOMETIMES IT TAKES LOSING
EVERYTHING TO FIND YOURSELF

JULIANA BUHRING

W. W. NORTON & COMPANY

INDEPENDENT PUBLISHERS SINCE 1923

NEW YORK LONDON

Frontispiece courtesy of the author.
Map © Liane Payne/www.lianepayneillustration.co.uk.

Printed in the United States of America
First Edition

For information about permission to reproduce selections from this
book, write to Permissions, W. W. Norton & Company, Inc.,
500 Fifth Avenue, New York, NY 10110

For information about special discounts for bulk purchases, please
contact W. W. Norton Special Sales at specialsales@wwnorton.com
or 800-233-4830

Manufacturing by Quad Graphics Fairfield
Book design by Barbara Bachman
Production manager: Louise Mattarelliano

ISBN 978-0-393-29255-8

W. W. Norton & Company, Inc.
500 Fifth Avenue, New York, N.Y. 10110
www.wwnorton.com

W. W. Norton & Company Ltd.
Castle House, 75/76 Wells Street, London W1T 3QT

1 2 3 4 5 6 7 8 9 0

To Hendri Coetzee, *who inspired a dream,*
and Antonio Zullo, *who helped me realize it.*

People say that what we're all seeking is a meaning for life. I think that what we're really seeking is an experience of being alive.

JOSEPH CAMPBELL

The Route

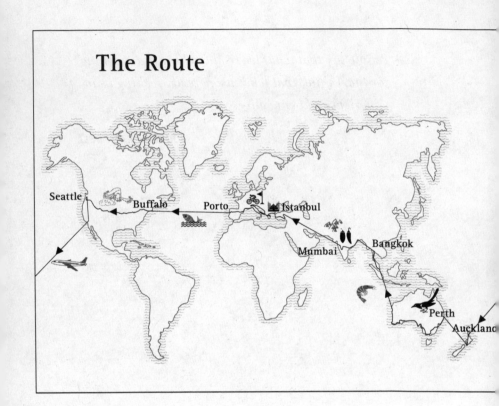

CONTENTS

THIS ROAD I RIDE

PROLOGUE

A noisy crowd of cyclists and motorcyclists has gathered outside the bar in the small town of Cardito on the periphery of Naples. Everybody wants to take pictures, but what I really want is a good espresso. "There are groups of cyclists waiting to meet you along the way," Antonio says into my ear, checking his watch as I knock back a shot of rich, fragrant coffee at the bar. It's a typical Neapolitan bar selling warm *cornetti*, lottery tickets, and cigarettes, with harsh fluorescent lighting and a small flat-screen TV airing a soccer match. I couldn't be happier. How I've missed a decent Neapolitan espresso over the last five months!

"People will try and stop you to take pictures, but you've just gotta go. There's no time. Remember, it's important you don't stop. Midday you *must* be in Piazza del Plebiscito." As my logistics manager, Antonio has absorbed most of the stress of my eighteen-thousand-mile around-the-world cycle ride. He has not had a good night's sleep since the start of the endeavor and looks to have matched my own weight loss pound for pound. His curly black hair is unbrushed, and his tired eyes, often squinting as though deep in thought, are hidden behind dark Ray-Bans. He had little idea what he was signing up for when he agreed to manage the logistics for my journey just over a year ago. Then again, neither did I. The finish line cannot come soon enough for either of us.

"Okay, I'm ready. Where's Pegasus?" I haven't seen my bike since Antonio took it off to the garage for safekeeping yesterday. His younger brother, Riccardo, wheels it over, filthy from yesterday's rain, dry mud crusted along the white carbon frame. The seat leather is torn in places, and there are dents and scratches on the paint, but considering the mileage it has done, Pegasus is in fairly good condition. For all the breakdowns and problems, it has gotten me around the world. I stroke the handlebars lovingly. This bicycle was my companion on the road for 152 days. I've talked to it a lot. "One last ride, Pegasus," I mumble now.

The waiting cyclists mount their bikes, and the motorcyclists rev their engines to "I Will Survive" blasting from a speaker strapped to one of the pillions. Antonio jumps into his blue Renault Clio, just ahead of us. People are whistling and clapping from the street, the apartment windows, and the balconies, shouting, "*Vai, Julie!*" Eager to escape from all the noise and attention, I clip into the pedals and push off.

Our procession grows along the last forty miles into Naples. Cyclists from Schiano, the company that donated my bike, join us. We head toward the bike shop, Cicli

Caputo, where I first learned how to change a tube and dis-assemble Pegasus. The shop's cyclists, whom I joined on training rides just eight months ago, are waiting for us there. We're now over fifty strong: teenage boys and older seasoned cyclists, amateurs and professionals, all accompanying me to the finish line. The police are on the streets to hold back the traffic as we pass.

The motorcade, blowing musical horns, blocks cars at the junctions so we never have to stop. The atmosphere is jovial. The sun breaks through the clouds as we crest Pozzuoli, where ruins of the former Roman port city mingle with modern apartment complexes. The ocean below is silver gray, the city of Naples a colorful tangle of buildings under the shadow of Vesuvius. I laugh with euphoria and shout to the guys pedaling next to me, "What a beautiful day to ride!" They nod and give me the thumbs-up.

More cyclists are waiting for us farther along the road: casual biking commuters and several women from the Green Cycle community. The pace slows to accommodate everyone as our ranks continue to swell. The last miles leading to Piazza del Plebiscito follow the new bicycle path along the waterfront and into the city center. The entourage disperses into the waiting crowd of friends and online followers as I pedal across the cobbled square and over the finish line. A Neapolitan flag is thrown around my shoulders. People are clapping and shouting "Brava!" A makeshift stage has been set up, and someone is standing on it, shouting into a microphone, "Juliana is baaaaaack!"

Antonio is waiting for me as I climb off my bike, and I

give him a giant hug. *"Brava*, baby!" he says, pinching my cheek affectionately, as he often does. *We* did it! It is his victory as much as mine. I may have done the pedaling, but he has done everything to ensure I could.

I'm led onto the stage with Pegasus, and a microphone is thrust in front of my face. They obviously want me to say something, but my mind is blank. It all feels so surreal. I've made it around the world, and I can't quite believe it's really over. I can feel the bruised, shredded skin on my thigh from yesterday's fall. My toes are black and blistered with frostbite. My face is raw from sun- and windburn. My body is near collapse. In this moment, standing at the finish line with the crowd clapping and cheering, the difficulties, the sickness, the exhaustion, the cold, the hunger, the pain, and the tears seem like a dream, something that never really happened.

Yet it *did* happen, against everyone's expectations— without a sponsor or any funding, without a technical or medical support team, with only eight months of training on a bicycle. Nobody believed I would make it, certainly not all the way around the world, averaging 125 miles a day. I was not an athlete or a cyclist. There was nothing to qualify me for such a huge undertaking: nothing but willpower and the determination to finish, no matter what. I had set out to prove that anything is possible, that we can do things that are far bigger than ourselves.

D-DAY

The journey began five months earlier on a gray morning in late July. Weather reports had predicted rain, and heavy clouds were forming over the crowd of friends and curious strangers gathered in Piazza del Plebiscito, one of the largest squares in Europe. Hedged in by the imposing facade of the seventeenth-century Royal Palace on one side and the neoclassical church of San Francesco di Paola on the other, Naples's central piazza seemed a natural starting point for my adventure.

"Are you ready?" Antonio asked, pushing through the crowd of well-wishers, photographers, and journalists who were waiting to see me off. The question was hypothetical, of course. Could one ever be "ready" for something like this? According to general opinion, I was not. All I had were a few thousand euros, a bike, and a dream.

A dream that was born out of grief. The kind of grief that

makes you older and sadder—or that changes you, becoming an impetus for random yet life-changing acts.

I had first met Hendri Coetzee eight years earlier at the Rock Garden nightclub in Kampala. I was standing with my back against the bar, half-painted by the neon lights, talking with a group of friends. Hendri was sipping a vodka Red Bull at the edge of the darkness when our eyes caught and locked together for what seemed like a very long time. It was as though he had no desire or intention to interrupt this unexpected meeting by looking away. How well I remember those eyes—clear blue orbs even in the murky light of the club. Slowly he moved toward me, never breaking eye contact, till our faces were just inches apart.

"You can't take your eyes off me," I whispered.

"And you are just dying to kiss me," he answered.

If another word was spoken, I don't remember it. Our hands, co-conspirators to our eyes, found each other. We walked into the darkness without another word, away from the drunken crowd of regulars. Nobody and nothing else existed in that moment.

Hendri was an explorer whose journeys had included walking over a thousand miles down the East African coast, numerous missions through the uncharted wilds of the continent, and source-to-sea expeditions down the courses of the White and Blue Niles. He jokingly called himself the "Great White Explorer." I preferred the "River God," and if you had seen him agilely navigating down grade-five rapids in his orange Fluid kayak, you would understand why.

Our subsequent encounters were similarly brief and intense, without any expectation of a future together, lasting only in a series of perfect, flawless moments that, like our first meeting, always felt a bit surreal. He was working as a raft guide for a kayaking company in Jinja, taking people down the Nile's whitewater rapids. I was living in Kampala, a quasi-missionary by day, when I would distribute food and medical supplies to orphanages and schools, and a go-go dancer at night, performing in a professional dance troupe to pay the bills. Hendri had heard there were foreign girls dancing at the Rock Bar and had come there with a friend to watch us dance some weeks before our first meeting.

The last time I saw him in person, he was preparing to lead another 4,200-mile Nile source-to-sea expedition, following in the path of the American explorer John Goddard. After he set off, my life took a dramatically different turn. I left Kampala, wrote a book, and became somebody else. We lost contact for several years.

I was in London, visiting a friend who had also lived in Kampala, when I saw Hendri's profile on her Facebook page. I sent him a friend request, and he answered immediately.

"Well I'll be. Never for one second did I think I would ever hear from you again. Was just thinking about you a few weeks ago. Pleasantly, I might add."

He had just returned from a solitary expedition through the Congo and was finding it difficult to reintegrate into "normal life." Never quite belonging anywhere myself, I understood the feeling. We began corresponding regularly. It was as if no time had passed and a lifetime had passed. A lot had changed in our lives over the preceding five years, but almost nothing had changed between the two of us.

The subject of freedom was an important one for both of us, and while we had gone after it in very different ways, our respective searches had led to similar conclusions. "You spoke to me of freedom some time ago," he wrote early on in our correspondence, after he had bought and read my first book, which detailed my childhood growing up in the infamous cult the Children of God. The message continued:

> I didn't know how serious an issue it is for you. Viktor Frankl is my favorite psychologist. He says, *We can achieve meaning through work, love, or suffering.* Perhaps those who suffer most have the best chance to find meaning. You will be in a better position than myself to answer that. Frankl sums up with *suffering is inevitable* and states that *the last of the human freedoms is to choose your reaction to your suffering.* As someone who has searched for freedom from who knows what his entire life, I am positive it's the hardest freedom to achieve.

Every email and message we exchanged was like water for a parched wanderer. They called to the wild in me, the rebel, the social outsider. Although we were continents apart, I valued his words more than anyone else's. Even if all we ever shared was a distant friendship, that was worth more to me than a hundred close acquaintanceships.

Things sped up quickly within a few short months, as though we both sensed time was short, rushing toward some unknown collision with fate.

"I think we both know that perhaps me and you are only a symptom, neither of us a cause, for this attraction," he wrote in one email.

That we seek each other in desperation, an outside chance that someone who is unlike the others could be the thing we are looking for, having searched everywhere else—a last resort. For us who run at things, the fear of testing such a theory could be painful. For us, slow and tentative is hard. Intensity flows thick in our veins. Still, I think we have things to tell each other and things to share. We are under each other's skin.

He was planning another expedition with two American kayakers, paddling down one of the least explored rivers in the Congo. He would be back for New Year, so I booked a flight to Uganda for December 30, 2010. We had decided to meet up and see what happened.

On December 3 I logged into Skype to find him online, waiting for me.

Hendri: I was just thinking about you.
Juliana: I just had the sudden fancy that I should log on.

Hendri: Thank God.

Juliana: Where are you?

Hendri: In Kalemie, Congo. Been stuck for a few days. Waiting for some permissions to travel.

Juliana: But you still have access to the Internet! Well, go figure. Africa—contradiction in all things.

Hendri: Been thinking of you hard all day.

Juliana: Strange. So have I.

Hendri: When will I have the privilege?

Juliana: Of?

Hendri: You.

Juliana: I arrive on the 31st.

Hendri: If ever there was an incentive to survive a mission . . .

Juliana: You'd better. I'm waiting for you. A month seems like a very long time.

Hendri: Feeling close to you. Amazingly so. Just a few hippos and some savages between us. Will take care of it asap.

Juliana: Oh good. You work on that. And I'll work on getting myself over to you.

Hendri: Soon.

Juliana: Yes.

Hendri: This is probably the last time I will have Internet until the end of the trip. 3–4 weeks if all goes semi to plan.

Juliana: Please come back in one piece. I need all of you.

Hendri: And you shall have it.

Juliana: :)

Hendri: Sleep well. Dream of me. I will of you.

Juliana: I usually do. You are never far from my
thoughts.

Hendri: I'll let you know as soon as I'm back in
Uganda.

Juliana: Okay. Until then.

Hendri: Love and light.

Juliana: Safe journey, my River God.

I awoke on the morning of December 8 and logged into
Facebook while sipping a cup of coffee. The news feed was
filled with tributes to Hendri, punctuated with statements of
shock and disbelief. I frantically messaged a mutual friend:
"What the hell is going on? What's happened to Hendri?"

"He was paddling down the Lukuga River, the two
American kayakers he was with were just ahead of him,
when a giant crocodile came up out of nowhere and dragged
Hendri from his kayak. His body has not been found," our
friend informed me. "I'm still in too much shock to process
it right now. Hendri's always cheated death. I just can't
believe it's true."

I sat motionless, unable or unwilling to process any of it
either. Of course it was not true. He would crawl out of the
river somewhere with that cheeky smile of his, dragging a
fresh croc skin.

When the news finally sank in, I fell to pieces. The first
couple of days I stayed curled up in bed crying, calling his
name over and over as though by some miracle that would

bring him back. Sometimes when I thought there were no more tears left in my dry, swollen eyes, I'd think, *I'm better today. Today I will not cry.* Then something would trigger a memory, and I'd crumple over in a spasm of tears, the ground would blur, the world would spin, and I'd lose my breath.

Deep sorrow marks you more than any physical scar. After weeks of crippling grief, I woke up one morning, looked in the mirror, and knew I had to do something to save myself or be swallowed up by the profound melancholy I was drowning in. Death has a way of putting the temporary nature of life into sharp perspective, reminding you that time is always racing toward that one inevitability, inspiring an urgency to do everything now, quickly, while you still can.

What started as an act of desperation soon became an all-consuming purpose, one that really began the night after Hendri's memorial. I caught the flight I'd booked to Uganda and arrived, as originally planned, on December 31. Then I joined his family and friends on the banks of the Nile a month to the day after his death, to commemorate the life of the man we had all loved.

"Perhaps he could not have gone any other way. Hendri would have been furious if he'd died in his bed," one of his closest friends commented.

A few of us were sitting around a log table on the veranda of a layover house for kayakers and social misfits who were passing through Jinja. Hendri had stayed there himself for a time. Bamboo torches burning citronella kept the mosquitoes hovering on the periphery of our little circle of light.

The cicadas were chirping loudly. The African night is never silent.

"I want to do something big before I settle down," said a cute English blonde who had known Hendri only briefly.

Why must we settle down? I thought. *Why do we feel this is expected of us after a certain age?* I would be turning thirty in a few months' time. Did all women start a biological countdown at that point? Or was settling down just what all mature people did?

"Something like cycling across Canada," continued the blonde. Then she turned toward me. "Would you want to do it with me? It wouldn't be too hard to find sponsors if we did it for some charity. We could raise the money and just go."

"Maybe," I said. But the more I thought about it, the more bored I became with the whole idea. Why *Canada*? Why not somewhere else? Somewhere I had never been.

The idea continued to ferment after I returned home to Italy, so I started researching interesting cycle journeys on the Internet. It was not long before I stumbled upon Mark Beaumont's bicycle ride around the world. His solo journey, during which he covered 18,296 miles in 194 days, had been well documented by the BBC and other news outlets. A little knot of excitement twisted in my stomach. Now *that* would be the ultimate cycling adventure. The fact that I had never really ridden a bike would make the challenge greater, and the entire world more interesting.

When I first mentioned the idea to friends, I was met with either blank silence or incredulous laughter. The more they scoffed, the more determined I became. When an idea gets stuck in my head, it simmers for a while until I get either bored or motivated. But tell me it's impossible, and that four-syllable word sets me off like a trigger. Whenever I'm told I *can't* do something, a little voice in my head starts counting down, like in a missile launch: "In five . . . four . . . three . . . two . . . one . . . ignition . . ."

Antonio was one of the first people I told about this next big idea. We had hit it off instantly the moment I'd walked into his pub, the Hickory, shortly after arriving in Naples, and he had soon become my best friend and companion in most of my mad schemes. The general lawlessness of southern Italy had attracted the rebel in me, its weather closely mirrored its people with their fiery warmth, and the organized chaos seemed familiar, comfortable, almost like home. Not that I knew where or what "home" was. I had lived a nomadic life until that point. Settling in one place had always been difficult. It still is. Whenever I start to get comfortable anywhere, I also start to get itchy feet.

Meeting Antonio was a bit like finding family, which made me feel even more at home in Naples. *Family* do not have to be blood relatives. They are the people who support you through good times and bad, the people who know all your secrets, celebrate your highs, and stick around through the lows. You cannot choose your blood relatives, but you can choose your family. *There is a friend who sticks closer than a brother*, says a verse of Proverbs. For me, his name is Antonio.

He listened politely but did not take me too seriously at

first. Why would he? *I want to walk the road to Santiago* . . .
I want to drive a campervan across Alaska. . . . He had
heard plenty of grandiose talk before. This was just another
wacky notion that would soon vanish as soon as a shinier,
more fanciful dream took hold.

"Listen, we'll go on a cycling holiday this summer,"
Antonio suggested, believing this would be the cure for my
latest itch.

We got a couple of inexpensive touring bikes and pedaled
from Berlin to Copenhagen that August. It was a relaxed
cycling holiday, covering no more than 35 or 40 miles a day.
But I didn't want it to end and returned to Naples more
determined than ever.

As temperatures cooled in autumn after a scorching summer, I began to push my cheap touring bike out the door
every morning to "train myself." Antonio realized that this
was more serious than he had thought, and he immediately
set about talking me out of it.

"It's a nice idea, Ju," he said in one of our more serious
conversations, "but let's be realistic. It would take a cyclist
years to do something like that. And you are not even a
cyclist."

"I'll become one," I argued.

"You don't even have a good bicycle. Where are you going
to get the money from? It's expensive, even if you do it in the
cheapest possible way."

"I'll find a sponsor."

The conversation continued over the next few weeks.
After all the remonstrations, appeals to logic, and predicted

unhappy endings failed to dampen my determination, Antonio realized there was only one thing he could do: jump in the deep end with me and hope we didn't both drown. For this demonstration of supreme loyalty, he was awarded the uncoveted role of "logistics manager."

Researching around-the-world cycle journeys—from Nick Sanders, who set the original record in 1984, riding 13,000 miles in 78 days, to Vin Cox's 2010 record of over 18,000 miles in 165 days—I could find no mention of any woman ever attempting it. Out of curiosity, I sent an application to the Guinness World Records, stating my intention to circumnavigate the world by bike. Their response confirmed what I had already guessed: there was no women's record for circumnavigating the world by bike. That fact alone seemed odd to me. Was the world really so dangerous for women? Or were women physically unable to cycle the same distances at the same speeds as men? There was only one way to find out. I decided if I was going to be the first woman to cycle around the world, I might as well have a crack at the men's record while I was at it. Go big or go home, right?

The Guinness people sent me a long document containing a list of rules. I was required to cover a minimum of 18,000 miles solely by bike, in either an east-to-west or a west-to-east direction, while the total journey distance—including all transit by air or sea—had to be a minimum of 24,900 miles. The ride had to start and finish in the same place and pass at least two antipodal points (two places that line up through the earth's center). The clock would stop the moment I reached an airport or port to cross an ocean or some other impassable barrier, such as a war zone, and would start again upon landing at the next destination. The same bicycle had to be used throughout the attempt, but repairs could be made and replacement parts fitted in the event of mechanical failure. Satellite tracking was required, and a daily logbook with signatures of dignitaries and people I met on the road, photographs taken at strategic points, and receipts would all be collated as evidence.

Since there had never been a women's record, I decided to try to beat the current men's best time of 165 days. This would mean pedaling an average of 110 miles every day for more than five months. For someone who had never cycled seriously before, or even done much sport of any description over the previous decade, the physical challenge alone was monumental. Puttering around the school playground on training wheels as a six-year-old in the Philippines and my weeklong Germany–Denmark holiday with Antonio were the sum total of my pedaling experience. And I knew next to nothing about bike technology or the science of cycling.

No matter. How hard could it be? I jumped into the challenge—or rather mounted it—with great enthusiasm, cycling whenever I had any spare time, riding around the streets of Naples and beyond on my heavy touring bike, wearing ordinary gym shoes. Each day I upped the mileage a little more. My optimism took me a long way, like the bumblebee who, ignorant of the fact that physicists say she should not be able to fly, flies anyway. Within two months, I was pedaling seventy-five miles on a ride without much difficulty.

———

The second—and far greater—obstacle was financial. I sent out sponsorship requests to every major sports company, both in Italy and abroad. Most never bothered replying. Those who did gave the standard "not interested, but good luck" response. No doubt my endeavor seemed so out there that it wasn't even worth considering. I had no background in endurance sport. There was nothing to qualify me for such a huge undertaking.

After many discouraging responses from the big brands, Antonio started sending out emails to smaller, local companies. The first—and only—positive reply came from Mario Schiano. His family had been building bicycles in Naples for over three generations. Mario proposed a meeting to hear more about what I was planning and to discuss how they might help, so Antonio and I drove to the sprawling Schiano warehouse in Frattamagiore, on the periphery of Naples.

Mario was waiting for us when we arrived, and we followed him down a long, gray-tiled corridor to his office on the second floor. He lowered his tall, lanky frame into the chair at the head of the conference table and motioned for us to join him.

"So, tell me everything, from the beginning," he said.

I let Antonio, as the logistics manager, do most of the talking. Italian was not a language that came easily to me, and I lacked confidence in my ability to convey what I wanted to say. More to the point, in addition to owning the Hickory,

Antonio worked as a portfolio manager for a bank, so negotiating business matters was his forte. Not for the first or the last time, I was glad I had him at my side.

Mario listened carefully as Antonio outlined the plan. "So what exactly do you need from me?" he asked.

"I need a bike," I said before Antonio could answer.

"That's no problem. We can give you one."

And just like that, I had a bike.

"Do you have a trainer preparing you for the ride?" Mario asked.

"No. I've been training myself, alone, up to now."

"One moment." Mario dialed a number and spoke into the phone for several minutes. "Okay," he said, hanging up. "There's a sports trainer who specializes in training cyclists for races. His name is Professor Perna, and he says he can help with your preparation. Here's his number. You can even go there today if you like."

My new trainer's full name was Umberto Perna, but "Professor" had a 007 ring to it, so I called him that. An ex-cyclist now in his fifties, he agreed to see me, I suspect, more out of curiosity than anything else. He was on the lookout for me from the window of his gym when I drove up for our appointment the next day and motioned for me to come through the side gate.

"*Ciao, Juliana!*" He met me at the entrance and kissed both my cheeks in the usual Mediterranean greeting. His bright blue eyes, thin lips, and long Roman nose all seemed remarkably familiar.

"You look like someone I know," I said, then spent the next few minutes trying to work out who it was. Finally I had it. "*Sean Penn!* You could easily be his brother. You know—the actor?"

"Ah, *sì*. You think so?" He seemed pleased. The ice was broken, and we sat down to the serious business of plotting world domination by bicycle.

"Mario told me a little bit about your plan. You want to cycle around the world, yes? When are you planning to leave?"

"In around four months, I hope."

"Ah!" He threw up his hands. "Then we've got time."

While I hardly shared his optimism, his confidence in my athletic potential was reassuring. Or perhaps he was being ironic and I failed to notice. Either way, at that point the interrogation really got rolling.

"How long have you been cycling?"

"Well . . . give or take . . . a couple of months."

"How many miles are you currently able to cycle?"

"At the moment, around a hundred twenty a day."

The Professor grunted and raised an eyebrow in surprise. "Which shoes are you using?"

"Uh, these." I pointed to the trainers I was wearing.

"You've been cycling in *those*?"

I could see by the look on his face that that was not the right answer.

The rest of the interview didn't last long. The Professor's parting instructions were simple: "Get your pedals changed to clips. Get shoes with cleats. Then come back here when you've got both."

I bought a pair of mountain bike shoes, changed the pedals, and cycled with them the very next day, wondering what all the fuss was about. Cleats were supposed to improve performance significantly, but the only immediate difference I felt was the panic of being stuck to the bike, unable to eject my foot in an emergency. And there are always plenty of emergencies when cycling around Naples, a city infamous for its careless, lawless drivers and chaos on the roads.

Just a few weeks into my training, an eight-wheel freight truck clipped me as I negotiated a bend on a narrow road. I did a tumbleweed flip-roll-roll, landing unceremoniously on my bum. The truck sped on. There were a few moments of shock, followed by fury that the truck driver hadn't stopped. When the adrenaline spike wore off, the pain kicked in. I went to the hospital for scans to make sure no damage had been done to my head. It turned out that I had gotten off lightly with just a few scrapes and bruises, a twisted wrist, and a very sore neck.

Later came the inevitable moment of reflection and re-evaluation as I assessed the potential dangers of cycling the world alone. The next time I was the victim of a hit-and-run driver, I could be in Turkey or India, far from help and home.

"Aren't you afraid?" a friend had asked just a week before the accident.

"Afraid of what?"

"That something will happen to you out there, when you're all alone."

There is always something to be afraid of in this world, but fearing the unknown seems a futile waste of energy. One can plan for every potential risk, possibility, and eventuality, but if a truck is going to hit you, all the planning in the world won't make any difference. Of course, the alternative would be to stay at home, in the safety and predictability of a familiar environment, and never venture far for fear of myriad dangers. But then none of us would do anything at all, and what would be the point of being alive?

Hendri had written a lot about fear whenever he confronted it before embarking on a mission. Now his words assumed new significance for me:

> So much of life is spent doing arbitrary tasks and fearing things that will never happen. During expeditions you get to live the extraordinary. Dealing with fear is the price you pay to be able to achieve peak experiences and learning. Nothing great can be achieved without jumping the fear barrier.

I was well beyond jumping that barrier. This whole endeavor felt close to free-falling over a cliff without a parachute. Yet I didn't feel afraid. So many people asked why I wanted to cycle around the world. I never really had a satisfactory answer. Maybe on some deep, subconscious level, it was a journey from which I did not intend to return. After Hendri, I had nothing left to lose.

I went back to the Professor a week later, ready for my transformation into a lean, mean cycling machine. There were newspaper cuttings on the wall of his office among photos of his family and friends. One showed a much younger, more muscular version of the Professor on a sleek racing bike. He had been the champion of Campania in his younger years.

I pointed at the picture and asked, "How many miles was this race?"

"Seventy-five." He seemed pleased I had noticed that he was the cyclist. "Cycling was different in the old days. Those of us who trained wanted only one thing in life: to cycle. My trainer was a legend. He knew how to make a cyclist out of anyone. The youth these days . . ." He shook his head.

"What's changed?"

"They don't want to make the necessary sacrifices. Their parents have money, they can have whatever they want, so they have no need for challenges. Why struggle for a dream when you can live the good life without the work?"

I couldn't help thinking, *But where is the satisfaction in achievement without struggle?*

"The best cyclists, those who become champions, are the ones who come to me with nothing, from poor families, without a future. Then cycling becomes everything to them, a lifestyle. They'll sacrifice anything for it. That's the only way to achieve anything important."

The Professor's first order of the day was to adjust my seat and handlebars to ensure maximum comfort, as I had been experiencing tension in my middle back and knees during long hours on the bike. Then he measured, weighed, pulled, and stretched me before finally drawing up my new training regime. I needed to bulk up a few more pounds before setting off, he said, because I'd lose both weight and muscle during five months of cycling.

"Building physical endurance means more than just being able to cycle for many hours," he explained. "You need to build some muscular strength and speed."

His plan for the next couple of months involved three days' cycling, two jogging, and two in the gym training and building muscle each week. Then I would gradually add more cycling while reducing everything else over the next two months, until I was doing at least eight hours nonstop on the bike most days.

"Call me anytime you feel the program is getting too easy, and I'll add more. But listen to your body. Only you know what you're capable of."

I liked the Professor. He dropped morsels of wisdom every time he spoke.

"*In bocca al lupo!* [Into the mouth of the wolf!]," he called to me on my way out the office. It's an old Neapolitan adage for good luck.

I followed the Professor's advice to the letter: I cycled, I ran, I lifted weights. I would get up at the crack of dawn—a challenge in itself, since I'm usually a night owl and have difficulty waking up early. Cold December mornings made it even harder to drag myself from under the cozy warmth of the duvet at six a.m.

Because cycling anywhere within Naples is an ordeal in itself, what with the crazy drivers and poorly maintained roads, I would put the bike on the rack on the back of my car and drive an hour into the countryside. During the week, I taught English at a private school in the afternoons and evenings, so I would cycle between four and five hours every morning. On weekends, the rides would be much longer.

I still secretly wondered whether the Professor truly believed I could make it around the world, or whether he had taken me on as a charity case. Either way, if I was willing to put in the hard graft, I knew he would do his bit to give my training structure and focus. Maybe he was curious to see how far I would get. It was rare to find a woman interested in cycling in southern Italy, and the Professor had certainly never trained one before, much less for an endeavor of this magnitude.

"Remember, even if you don't make it all the way around, at least you will have tried something nobody else has done," he told me.

Even if you don't make it all the way around. I was hearing this ever more often. Apparently the prevailing opinion was that I would give it my best shot, fail, then come home to a supportive "It's better to have tried and failed than never to have tried at all"—a saying that tends to be most used by those who have never actually tested it.

A well-known bike shop, Cicli Caputo, became a favorite haunt. The owner, Mauro Caputo, was another friend of Mario Schiano. He let me hang around in the workshop and taught me basic repairs, like how to change tubes, chains, and brake pads. Meanwhile Mario built me a sophisticated touring bike, complete with suspension, disc brakes, and ample space for a rack over the rear wheel. Mauro assembled it and made the necessary size adjustments.

The Professor kept adding miles to the training plan and tweaking it in other ways. After five months I was pedaling his target of 110 miles five days a week.

"Physically you are ready," he told me in June. "I cannot do any more to prepare you."

I may have been physically ready, but I was completely unprepared in every other way. I still had not found a sponsor, which was hardly surprising, as nobody believed I would make it all the way around. And why would anyone invest in almost inevitable failure? I had originally intended to set off in April but delayed my departure in the hope of securing funding that never arrived. I could feel my resolve weakening as each day ticked by. If I didn't leave soon, I knew I never would. So ready or not, I chose July 23 as my departure date and vowed to stick to it.

Then on July 11 I received an email from Guinness World Records, informing me of a change in the rules.

Dear Record Attempter,

We are writing you to let you know that after much discussion within the Guinness World Records Records Management Team (RMT) regarding the records for "fastest circumnavigation by bicycle, true," (male) and (female), Guinness World Records has decided it will now recognize records only for full trip duration (including transfers, rest time, etc.) and not specifically for cycling time only.

As no female record has been set in this category, there is

no previous attempt to surpass. However, the time require-
ment acceptable for any successful first attempt is now 150
days, with a minimum total distance cycled of 18,000 miles
(28,970 km) and the total distance traveled by the participant
exceeding an equator's length, i.e. more than 24,900 miles
(40,075 km).

This decision was made after much deliberation and discussion internally within Guinness World Records and with
external consultants. We feel this decision will add more unifor-
mity to all attempts and also maintain the spirit of circumnavigation records, aligned with the remainder of our database.

We apologize for any inconvenience, but thank you for your
understanding and wish you luck with your record attempt!

I was floored. It made no sense. None of the men's records
had been completed in less than 150 days' *cycling* time—let
alone *total* time, including transits, which was what Guinness was now demanding. So why were they imposing this
new stringent time constraint for the first women's record? I
could only surmise that whoever had written the new rules
either did not know what they were talking about, or that
women were being held to higher physical standards than
their male predecessors. In order to ride eighteen thousand
miles within the new time frame, I would have to cycle, on
average, almost 125 miles every day. There would be no rest
days. And I would have to catch the earliest possible flight
whenever I arrived at an airport, and begin pedaling the
moment I collected my bike from the carousel.

I emailed Guinness, asking for the reasoning behind a

rule change that seemed to apply solely to my attempt. Receiving no reply, I called both the UK and US headquarters and was passed around between a number of officials within the organization. Nobody could give me a straight answer. It appeared that 150 days had been chosen simply because it was a nice round figure that sounded good to someone who had no idea what it signified in reality.

Apparently, though, I was not the only one kicking up a fuss about the rule change. A week later, just five days before my scheduled departure date, I received a second email:

Dear Record Attempter,

After many enquiries and comments from participants (both male and female) regarding the time established for the female category of 150 days being too difficult, we at Guinness World Records have decided to change it to **175 days or less**.

Thank you and good luck with your record attempt!

Yours sincerely,
Guinness World Records

At least this was more realistic and gave me a bit of breathing room in case of sickness or missed flights. The obstinate side of me could not let it go, though. If they wanted 150 days, then that was the target I would set myself. However, to achieve it, I would need a new strategy.

I decided to change from the comfortable but heavy hybrid I'd been training on to an ultra-lightweight carbon-fiber road bike. I would need to clock up maximum mileage in the shortest possible time. If I wanted the record, I would have to fly. Everything had to be light and aerodynamic. "Can you build me a bike that weighs no more than fifteen pounds?" I asked Mario. Working with Mauro, he designed and built a sleek white machine whose frame weighed in at just fifteen pounds.

I ditched the bike rack and the big saddlebags and ordered a small, light pack that attached directly under the seat, shaped like the abdomen of an insect. I planned to carry only the most basic essentials, aiming for a total weight of just forty-four pounds, so I had to pack smart. My saddlebag held a change of cycling clothes, two pairs of socks, a rain jacket, a pair of gloves, a T-shirt, mid-calf-length trousers, and a small toiletry bag containing deodorant, toothbrush, toothpaste, sunblock, and face cream. The middle frame bag was packed with tools, spare tubes, and other maintenance items. Finally a small handlebar bag held a first aid kit, medicine, and vitamins. A GPS Spot tracker attached to the bike frame would send regular updates of my speed, mileage, and current location to the website I had set up. This would allow Antonio to track my progress even if I was out of phone range. To reduce the risk of that, I would carry two phones with me: a strong, clunky little Nokia with my usual Italian number, and a smartphone that I would use with a local SIM card from whichever continent or country I was traveling through at the time.

Any number of problems, mechanical breakdowns, weather changes, or other unforeseeable events could ruin a day's ride, which meant that booking flights or accommodations more than a day or two in advance was impossible. Each day would be a fresh adventure, and I would never know exactly where I would end up that night.

My original route plan had been to head east, toward Asia, which had been the direction chosen by almost every other world cyclist. Apparently the winds tend to be more favorable in the direction of the earth's rotation. But the delays to my departure meant it now made more sense for me to head west and hit North America first. Given the choice between cycling through the Asian monsoon or into a headwind, I chose the latter.

Just a few weeks prior to my final departure date, I had still raised only around four thousand euros for the journey. The majority had been donated by a few close friends as well as Antonio and his partners from the Hickory. Most of my online supporters, who followed my preparations and offered to meet me on the road or put me up along the way, were people who, like me, had been born and raised in cults. We call ourselves "ex-kids."

I grew up in the notorious religious cult called the Children of God. It was founded in 1968 by a failed preacher who gathered together a motley following of disillusioned hippies in Huntington Beach, California, by preaching "revolution for Jesus" and "let's break away from the system." My parents' generation had wanted freedom from society, so they set about building their own utopia, then, ironically, imprisoned themselves and their children inside it. By the time I was born in 1981, the cult had spread to over one hundred countries and it boasted forty thousand "members," at least half of whom were children born and raised within the group. My childhood was an isolated existence spent behind high walls, in a world dominated by rules, restrictions, nos, don'ts and you-musts. My future was meticulously planned and preordained, my own desires and dreams sacrificed for the greater good of the group. Born into my parents' one-size-fits-all solution to life's problems, over time I naturally came to question their version of truth.

A utopian society works only when everybody shares the same aspirations, and the larger the population grows, the more unlikely that becomes. Thus, to control dissenters, the society becomes a dystopian dictatorship. I was quickly branded a rebel, and rebels never fare well in someone else's utopia. For this crime, I underwent a multitude of punishments in an attempt to "retrain me"—in other words, to break my mind and my will. In the land of shining happy people, I lived on the fringes with the other outcasts who dared to question the rules and the ideology. The more they tried to pound me into their mold, the more I rebelled.

Ever since I could remember, I had thought about escape. I used to sit on the rooftops watching the birds and envy their wings. I always carried within me the desire to know, to experience, to see beyond the confines of the bubble in which I grew up. While I did not know what I wanted or even expected from life, I did know that my parents' dream was not it. I yearned for the freedom to follow my own path and make my own choices. I wished my younger siblings would be allowed to do the same.

In 2004, not long after my eldest sister, Celeste, left the group, I made up my mind to follow her lead. The two of us and another sister who had managed to escape earlier, Kristina, then wrote a book, *Not Without My Sister*, which exposed the abuses and lack of fundamental human rights we had suffered when growing up in the Children of God. We established a charity that eventually merged with the Safe Passage Foundation, a not-for-profit organization founded and run by ex-kids that provides resources, support, and advocacy for others who find themselves alone, clueless, and grossly unprepared for life in the "outside world."

One problem many ex-kids encounter when trying to integrate into mainstream society has been the idea, promoted by irresponsible sections of media, that children who have suffered abuse are inevitably and permanently "damaged." It's a stigma that ex-kids carry like a moldy coat that can't be removed. In fact, most ex-kids hate being defined by the usual assumptions that accompany the "cult" label.

There are few questions I find more difficult to answer than the common polite inquiry "Where are you from?" because I dread the exchange that inevitably follows when I truthfully answer, "Nowhere."

"Oh, come on! Everyone's from somewhere."

"I'm not."

"Be serious now. What nationality are you?"

"German."

"So you're from Germany. Whereabouts in Germany?"

"I don't know. I never lived there. I got my mother's nationality."

"Where were you born, then?"

"Greece. But I never lived there, either."

"Well, where did you grow up then?"

"Everywhere. In over thirty countries across Asia, Africa, and Europe."

"Oh, right. I guess you really are from nowhere!"

Even that is only half the truth, though. The whole truth is just too much when meeting someone for the first time. It's simpler for ex-kids to assume new identities, invent new backgrounds, try to pretend we're anything but what we really are, because we refuse to let our pasts define who we are and who we want to become.

It takes courage and a certain mental toughness to leave behind everything you know. To walk away from your family, your friends, and your identity and start again with nothing, without any money or possessions, without a formal education or even basic knowledge of simple things like how to open a bank account, write a check, compile a CV, or apply for college. Few people know what it means to start life over from scratch. When you reject everything that was your life, discard everything you knew, and lose everything you loved, believed in, and lived, when you uproot yourself and turn against your own identity, when finally there is nothing left to lose, you lose the fear of loss itself, and that is perhaps the greatest self-emancipation one can experience. Many of my ex-kid friends are some of the strongest, most self-aware and empathetic people I know.

If we are the sum total of our experiences, then if anything, a childhood growing up without parents and moving constantly taught me independence, self-reliance, and adaptability. I have a really tough head on my shoulders, and I can endure a lot of pain, physical and mental. No wonder I felt up to the challenge of cycling around the world, no matter how arduous it might be. Hendri often said the strongest metals are forged through the hottest fires. That was where I planned to go: through the fire. To push my mind and body to their limits, to find out how far I could go and what I was capable of doing and enduring. Maybe at the end of it all I would find some kind of self-realization, or maybe I would still be as clueless as ever. Ultimately, though, the finish line was not the objective. It was all about the ride.

Pegasus, as I christened my new white stallion, arrived, and Mauro assembled it in his little shop. I had ten days in which to learn how to ride this ultra-light road bike. The riding position was entirely different from that of the hybrid; it felt awkward and unstable at first. I went out with Mauro's cycling team in a bid to improve my technique. The older cyclists in the group patiently followed close behind and gave helpful tips, such as the best positions for different terrain, how to stand on the pedals, and when to hold on to the middle of the handlebars on the uphill sections. Pegasus and I wobbled down the roads and took a few tumbles. In the unforgiving chaos of the Neapolitan traffic, I was like a baby deer just finding its legs in a stampeding herd of buffalo. It felt less about improving my poor bike-handling skills than about getting really good at falling.

Mauro joined me on a couple of rides so he could assess my riding position and cycling technique. His final diagnosis was grim, but he didn't have the heart to tell me in person, so he pulled Antonio aside instead. "Juliana isn't ready," he said. "It takes time, years even, to become a good cyclist. She can't possibly cycle around the world the way she rides now. If I were you, I would convince her to wait a year." Antonio dutifully passed on the message.

"By the time I come back, I will be a good cyclist," I told him. But I was thinking, *If I come back*.

Darker thoughts of this nature clouded most of the days leading up to my departure. The whys, hows, and what-ifs crowded my waking thoughts. At night I slept fitfully, disturbed by strange, ominous dreams. In one, I tried and failed to defuse a bomb that was about to explode. Seconds before the detonation, my final thought was: *I wonder if my consciousness will survive, or if it will be as though I never existed? At least now I'll find out.* Then there was a roaring explosion, and I felt my body disintegrate until I was nothing but ash that blew away in the wind. I was air and formless, without any of my senses, yet somehow aware that *if I'm having this thought right now, I must still exist.* Another night I found myself floating, weightless, looking down on the room and my own sleeping body.

Perhaps my subconscious was taking on the introspection and self-doubt I tried not to entertain as the unknown loomed ever closer. The reality of what I was about to undertake had started to sink in, and despite all my bravado, I was full of doubt. Did I have what it would take to pull this off? I couldn't believe I had gotten as far as I had. They say half the race is getting to the starting line. It certainly felt that way.

I had spent eight months planning and training for D-Day, but when it finally arrived, I was simply relieved not to have to think about it anymore. Friends kept asking me if I was *emozionata* (excited), but I felt only calm detachment, a cessation of thought, silence in my head. There was no more questioning of myself or my motives for going. I could not be any more or any less prepared. This was it. There could be no turning back now.

There was a sense of finality to all my actions this morning. The end of something rather than the beginning. Rolling out of bed, packing up my gear, locking my apartment door—all were performed like last rites. I knew that if something were to happen and I didn't make it back, it might well have been the last time that I did any of them. The finish line is in some relative future, reliant on many obscure *if*s. All I know for sure is that in less than an hour, I will clip in to my bike and pedal out of Naples.

Mario is already at the piazza with his family and staff, setting up the start line. TV cameras and reporters are arriving, drawn to the scene by the presence of the actress Maria Grazia Cucinotta, self-proclaimed patron of the event. The mayor, a couple of politicians from the Green Party, and a popular Neapolitan singer I've never heard of turn up for the photo op. I feel like a mascot everybody wants to pose with.

"Ju, it's almost eleven. Time to sign the logbook and leave." Antonio is standing at my elbow, experiencing enough nerves for both of us.

Pegasus and I have been adorned with an ample array of chili charms, the Neapolitan symbol of good luck. A cluster of tiny red peppers dangles from the handlebars, courtesy of the Professor. Others hang off my pockets and bike bags. I think, *If chili peppers attract luck as garlic wards off vampires, I should be well fortified against misfortune.*

Antonio hands me the blue leather-bound logbook, which the Guinness World Record rules stipulated I have to fill in daily. Opening the first page, I write at the head of four columns: "Date & Time," "Location," "Name," "Signature." The dignitaries and celebrities gather around to sign. It's all a bit surreal, as if it were happening around me, not to me. Cameras flash, a group of Schiano cyclists fall in behind, ready to escort me out of the city, and the crowd parts to make a path. Then, in one unanimous voice, the countdown begins.

"*Dieci . . . nove . . . otto . . . sette . . .*" I clip into the left pedal. "*Quattro . . . tre . . . due . . . uno . . . Vai!* Go Julianaaaaaa!"

I am off, out of the cobbled square, onto the Via Domiziana, the old Roman coastal highway leading out of the city. Only then do the threatening clouds explode. Pedaling through the deluge, I start to think, *What the hell have I gotten myself into?*

EUROPEAN CROSSING

The mountain refuge near Massa on the way to Genoa offers a comfortable bed and a hearty meal shared by guests at a long, rough wooden table. Italy is full of such *rifugi*, inexpensive mountain huts networked across the country. Spurred by enthusiasm and adrenaline, I've made good progress up the west coast from Naples, cycling four hundred miles in three days.

Tonight the fatigue has finally caught up with me, though. I feel like a zombie, watching platters of salami and prosciutto being passed around by a chirpy German family. Germans seem to turn up in the most unlikely places. The more abandoned and remote the village, the more likely you will find a random German traveler wandering through it. Only one or a couple, however. Equally bizarre is their absolute aversion to discovering other Germans within their immediate vicinity.

THIS ROAD I RIDE   39

"Feed the cyclist" is evidently tonight's theme. Giant portions of pasta and vegetables magically appear on my plate. I eat mechanically, more tired than hungry and mildly queasy from too much sun. Mediterranean summers are sweltering, and cycling through the midday heat is a torrid affair. Even after smothering factor-fifty sunscreen over my face and arms repeatedly, I was a fresh shade of crimson when I pulled up at the refuge earlier this evening.

The swarthy, bearded host ambles over as I'm polishing off the last strip of lasagne from my plate. "I hear you are cycling the world! Wonderful! I'm also something of an adventure enthusiast. I love if you tell me all about it over a bottle of fresh wine. Please, if you will join me at the other end of the table?"

As it turns out, he does most of the telling, which suits me fine. I'm too tired to talk. All I can think about is bed and how I might get into it. Pulling out a stack of yellowed magazines, he enthusiastically flips through the dog-eared pages bearing images of his youthful self, as he regales me with tales of his adventures traveling across Europe by donkey, horse, and Vespa.

"The donkey was my favorite of the three," he confides in a conspiratorial whisper that I half expect to end with *but don't tell the horse.* "A most reliable and hardy beast when it comes to crossing mountains."

The more wine he ingests, the more animated and verbose he becomes. At one point he whips out a guitar, and songs accompany his lively tales. The famous trans-European *burro* is summoned, and the poor beast is dragged from his repose in a nearby pen and led over to the dining table to receive a lyrical tribute from his master. The lengthy ballad describes his shiny black pelt, long ears, and white-rimmed eyes—accolades of less interest to the dumb beast than a nearby patch of juicy shrubs, which he is constrained from reaching till the end of the song.

I feel a bit like the donkey myself, wishing only for sleep but constrained by politeness to listen to the ramblings of my host. Fortunately the donkey, ignorant of social etiquette, does what I cannot and kicks up a fuss. It is with great relief that he at last reaches the weeds, and I my pillow.

JULY 28-29, 2012

After the first days of flat roads following the coast north toward Genoa, I hit my first major climb crossing the periphery of the Alps. It's not a high pass but still a long uphill slog of over twelve miles in punishing temperatures. Sweat stings my eyes, and my head feels like a pressure cooker ready to explode. I consume an entire water bottle hosing down my head and neck on the way up.

Pegasus starts to make clicking noises during the climb, and the clicking worsens after crossing the border into France at Ventimiglia. Worse, too, is the French coffee. I must stop expecting to find good espresso and be grateful for the important things, like law-abiding motorists. Unlike Italians, the French drive slowly and carefully, which may explain why I haven't seen much roadkill. I decide the amount of roadkill spotted per day is a good indicator of what to expect from a country's drivers. The Italian roads were riddled with dead cats and the occasional dog. France, apart from the odd hedgehog, has been relatively corpse free by comparison.

Cycling through the south of France is an unmitigated pleasure. I've settled into a comfortable rhythm, breaking every thirty miles for food and drink. The countryside is similar to that of northern Italy, only cleaner and more organized. Neat rows of vineyards pregnant with summer grapes, presided over by large farmhouses, dot the countryside, interrupted every now and again by quaint stone villages. The southern French are wonderfully friendly and accommodating. Although few speak English, they forgive my language deficiencies and rattle on helpfully in French, even when it's clear I can hardly understand a word.

Today the left-hand gear lever has stopped shifting altogether, so I'm forced to pedal on a single chainwheel until I reach a town with a bike shop. The balding mechanic in a black T-shirt with a print of bike parts arranged in the form of a skull shakes his head and clicks his tongue to imply it's serious. He removes my front derailleur to show me the damage: there's a hole right through the metal. I've no idea how I've managed to do that in just five days and a little over six hundred miles, but maybe I'm not using the gears correctly when climbing. As the bike was brand new when I set off, the gears and derailleur probably needed readjusting after a couple of hundred miles. But what do I know about bike mechanics? I'm just learning how to *ride* a bike properly! I had better figure it out soon, though. My cycling technique, or lack of it, will cost me in the long run. The mechanic removes the worn-out derailleur and replaces it with a secondhand part at the discounted cost of twenty euros. He works quickly, and I'm back on the road within half an hour. Still well within my projected time frame for reaching Avignon by sundown.

My sisters Mariana and Lily both live in the south of France, and they have offered beds en route, invitations I am grateful for in view of my limited finances. Free room and board are major perks of having seventeen siblings scattered across the globe. Our father believed in spreading love and truly practiced what he preached. By evolutionary standards, he was an outstanding success; when it came to caring for the offspring of his multiple partners, a resplendent failure. We siblings try to redress the imbalance by looking out for one another. Last night Mariana, who is older by a year, washed my smelly laundry, fed me steak, and let me crash on her bed in Antibes. Tonight I'm meeting Lily at the Gambrinus pub, her favorite watering hole in Avignon.

She is standing outside, waiting for me, as I ride up. "Juju!"

"Snork!"

Amid the long roster of half-siblings, Lily is my only full sister, though with our mutt mix of a gene pool, it's difficult to tell. I got the olive tones of a southern Mediterranean and the cheekbones of our paternal Polish grandmother, while

Lily has the pale Welsh complexion of our grandfather and the long, slender physique of an aristocrat. Her smattering of freckles and button nose enhanced her cheeky, playful character as a child. But it was probably her snore, something akin to the battle cry of an angry hippo, that inspired our brother Victor to call her Snorky. Over time she lost the cheek and the snore but the nickname stuck.

"I called up a local newspaper this morning when I knew you'd be passing through. The reporter's already here. I hope you don't mind."

While I stuff my face with a hamburger and chips, the journalist interviews me about the cycle. Too hungry to be polite, I answer between mouthfuls. *What is my route?* Heading for northern Spain. *Where did I set off from?* Naples. *How do I like Avignon?* It has a great art scene, and I loved coming for the Festival d'Avignon last year.

Once she leaves, I kick back with a beer and catch up with my sister. Similar in taste and thinking, yet polar opposites in character, we define that thin line between genius and crazy, she being the former. Although we take very different paths, we tend to arrive at the same conclusions, which could explain why we never disagree. Most of our lives have been spent apart. The cult leaders separated our parents when I was just four and Lily was still *in utero*, six months along. Mum was sent back to Germany with Mariana and our two-year-old brother, Victor, while I remained in the Philippines with foster carers. We met for the first time ten years later, I a gawky teenager and she a lanky nine-year-old with irregular teeth. Since then, whenever and wherever we happen to meet, it's always with the comfortable chemistry of two fish swimming in the affable current of instinctive camaraderie.

"You must be exhausted."

"I could sleep."

"I don't know how you're managing that much mileage every day."

"Neither do I. Hopefully I can sustain it."

"You're crazy."

"That is the general opinion."

When I ask for the bill, the pub owner's wife shakes her head vigorously, beaming smiles, and says something quickly in French.

"Your bill has already been paid for," Lily translates.

"By whom?"

Lily shrugs. "Don't worry. It's been taken care of."

I suspect my sister, of course.

"*Merci*," I tell the woman. "*Merci beaucoup*."

She kisses me three times, then presses seventy euros into my hand.

JULY 30, 2012

The unexpected donation from the proprietor of the Gambrinus pub is soon compounded by a second. Rising early the next morning, I discover an envelope slipped under the door from Lily's landlady, with another two hundred euros inside. These first acts of generosity, encountered less than a week into the cycle, are encouraging. Maybe I will manage to get around the world without a sponsor after all.

A few days ago I caught news of a forest fire raging through the Pyrenees on the French–Spanish border. Four dead and twenty-three injured. Unsure what to expect or whether it will be extinguished by the time I get there, I'm worried that I may have to change routes and make a detour.

The traffic appears to be running smoothly as I near the border at La Jonquera and nothing seems amiss. Only after crossing over do I get a vivid picture of the destruction that has swept through the Catalonian countryside. The landscape is a blackened carcass, the ground covered in powdery gray ash, mere charcoal stumps where thick forests stood just a week ago. The hollowed shells of ravaged homes dot the surrounding hills.

The devastation stretches on for at least ten miles before the terrain begins to normalize. It's clear how the fire spread so quickly. The north of Spain is dry, arid, and rocky, a semi-desert. The same monotonous Aleppo pine trees and thorny shrubs sprout from salmon shades of earth, interrupted every now and again by industrial-scale farmlands harvesting golden wheat. Temperatures rise to over a hundred degrees in the summer, and in areas with no wind, the heat can be suffocating. When the wind does blow, the strong, hot gusts carry the putrefying smell of fertilizer baking under the sun.

The road flattens out across the long, empty expanse of middle Spain. This leg of the trip is boring and uneventful, but at least I can pedal hard and fast. The audiobook of Tolstoy's ponderously long *War and Peace* has kept me company during the long hours in the saddle. With the winds mostly behind me, I've managed 175 miles on a couple of occasions, the most I've ever pedaled in a single day.

My goal is to reach Porto by 4 August. Just a day later tickets to the United States will almost double in price. In search of the fastest, most direct route, I cycle along the bigger highways and make good progress until two policemen in a Guardia Civil car pull me over. Neither speaks English, so I play the dumb foreigner. Their faces are stern as they give me what sounds like a stiff reprimand and motion for me to follow them off the highway. So now I have to stick to secondary roads, full of confusing detours and dusty roadworks.

As I near the Portuguese border, the local flora give the first clue of the strong headwinds I can expect: all the trees are bending distinctly eastward. And as the wind grows stronger, the terrain becomes hillier. Northern Portugal, I learn, is almost exclusively mountainous.

My last day in Europe, and I get off to a bad start. Cycling down a cobblestone street through the town of Bragança, the jolting dislodges my iPhone from its holder on the handlebars. The phone goes flying onto the cobbles, and I hear the crunch of glass as my wheels roll over it. The screen is cracked from top to bottom, but the phone still works, which is fortunate, since I can't afford a new one.

The Portuguese people have been delightful, far more relaxed than many of their Mediterranean counterparts. The food is hearty and plentiful—lots of meat, rice, and potatoes. I've been earning the extra calories. The final push toward Porto has been the toughest so far. The endless mountains and moments of exhaustion have had me close to tears, but the fatigue has been worth it. The higher I climb, the more incredible the views become. The setting sun casts deep shadows through the trees, offsetting radiant shades of pink and orange.

Despite the physical weariness of the climbs, I'm enthralled. This intense contrast of beauty and pain seem to make up the most poignant human experiences. Pain brings you to the basics of existence. It reminds you of your frailty, your mortality, your finiteness.

"If there was no suffering, man would not know his limits, would not know himself," says the British actor reading *War and Peace* in my earphones, as the fat, rich protagonist's view of life is slowly transformed on the battlefield.

His observations come at oddly appropriate times. I have decided to cycle the world to push my existence to its limit, to see what I am capable of, both physically and mentally. Pain puts you on a fast track to that realization. Pushing my legs up yet another mountain with the lactic acid building, my muscles cramping, and my lungs burning, it becomes a game of mind over matter. When I finally reach the top and look down at how far I've climbed, with the rolling mountains covered with pine trees and forest flora fading into the horizon, I want to laugh and cry and shout, *I am queen of the mountain!* It is a high that no drug can give you. I feel insurmountable and as powerful as a god.

"What more can one ask for in an adventure than to be moved by it?" Hendri once wrote, returning home from one of his many missions.

Yes! I think, smiling the whole way downhill, as the sun dips beneath the line of distant hills and disappears.

Spooning glutamine powder into my water bottle helps my muscles recover enough to take me the final thirty miles into Porto. It is ten p.m. and dark by the time I reach the city center in something of a daze, all energy reserves completely spent. I have just enough time to dismantle and box up Pegasus, eat two dinners, and catch the early morning flight to Boston.

I have covered 1,698 miles across western Europe in twelve days, pedaling an average of 142 miles a day. I know I cannot continue this pace indefinitely, but at least I have some extra miles in the bank for the down days that must inevitably come. Traveling across the United States has been high on my bucket list ever since reading Kerouac's *On the Road*, but never would I have imagined doing it on a bicycle. To say I'm excited is an understatement.

THE WRONG WAY

AUGUST 5–8, 2012

Tom reminds me of a more intelligent, real-life Homer Simpson. He is unaffected, big-hearted, loves Dunkin' Donuts and beer, and even works at a nuclear plant. His friends and family call him Uncle Shine, and the nickname could not be more fitting. Tom is a five-star guy. He befriended me on Facebook after reading my first book and has made a number of generous donations to the Safe Passage Foundation. On hearing I would be flying into his hometown of Boston, he decided to take some days off work to accompany me on the road by car. But that was the least of his contributions. He also sponsored my airline ticket and my first week's expenses in the States.

I found him in conversation with a couple of Irish lads at a bar in the Boston airport when I flew in a couple days ago and wheeled my boxed bike out of arrivals. The three of them greeted me with a beer. Tom had clearly wasted no time filling them in on the details of the record attempt.

"Hasn't anyone told you you're going the wrong way?" one of them said, on hearing that I was heading west to Seattle.

These words have already turned into a theme. Headwinds, and how to avoid cycling directly into them, have become my primary preoccupation. There is nothing more physically and mentally debilitating than pedaling against a headwind. It drains your morale, saps your energy, and makes you want to scream, weep, and beat the handlebars in frustration. I would choose a 20 percent gradient any day over a headwind. There is no arguing with the general opinion: where winds are concerned, I am definitely going the wrong way round.

My first day in America was a bleak mix of wind, hills, and rain. Pedaling through a downpour somewhere outside Boston, I got my first puncture. In the time it took to change the tube in the rain, two separate cop cars stopped to ask if I was okay within five minutes of each other. Passing motorists must have called 911, meaning I must have looked *in distress*. "You all right, ma'am?" asked the second cop. Wet, cold, and annoyed, definitely. But *all right*? Well, sure. He hovered, watching me work, helpless to help.

Tom drove up next and ambled out of the warmth of his car in a large blue tank top and shorts. He had noticed my tracker had stopped and backtracked to find me. Like the police, there was little he could do in the way of direct assistance, but in times of misery, a friendly face can be a game changer.

"Boy, you're gonna hate America by the time you leave," he said as I pumped the tire and slid the wheel back onto the bike. He was worried the brutal elements, the hills, and the punctures were giving me a negative impression of the country he loves.

"Hills, punctures, wind, and rain are standard fare the world over," I assured him.

Actually there is nothing standard about the amount of punctures I have already experienced in America. US highways are littered with metal shards from exploded truck tires. After battling headwinds, changing tubes has been the greatest time consumer. I need new tires, and that is not the least of my bike troubles. Since arriving, my right-hand gear shifter has been problematic, jumping between two extremes and forcing me to pedal in either the highest or the lowest gear.

In a bike shop the aging mechanic does not seem to know what he's doing. "Ah, this is the SRAM RED system. I'm not too familiar with these," he says, scratching his head. He gives it a look over and tries adjusting the cables, but the gears still jump. "Looks to me like you're gonna need to change the shifter," he tells me finally.

It's an expensive part—a minimum of six hundred dollars, which may as well be six thousand at this point. Unconvinced the problem merits such a drastic solution, I decide to keep pedaling till I find another bike shop and another mechanic's opinion.

Tom messaged Antonio to ask what I would need on the road, so his car is full of chocolate-covered dried fruit, energy bars, Gatorade, and bananas. *Bananas!* I hope I didn't offend him when I screwed up my nose and left him standing by the roadside when he held one out to me. There is only one fruit in the world I truly hate, and that happens to be the wonder food that most athletes swear by. The smell alone makes me gag. I could starve in a jungle full of banana plants. I don't think Tom minds too much when, at the next food stop, I tell him the bananas are all his.

AUGUST 10, 2012

Near Buffalo, New York, I say goodbye to Tom, who has to head back home, to his job in Boston. I'm sorry to see him go. He has become a great friend and champion of my cause. My impressions of America are formed from people like him, whose generosity smooths my path across their continent.

The scenery hardly changes throughout the northeastern states: cornfields on the right, wheat on the left, and a road cutting through the middle. Two little boys playing on a giant tractor, with dirty overalls and hay-colored hair, wave and shout, "Hey there, bicycle lady!" Farther down the road, I pass a horse-drawn wagon filled with Amish women in dark dresses and bonnets, heading into town to sell their organic produce. People riding lawn mowers raise a hand as I pedal by. A couple of Harley-Davidsons roar past. A man up a ladder is painting his wood-slate house white, the radio blasting "Let it Be." A red, white, and blue flag hangs from every porch. The wind is fresh, the sun is high. *This* is America.

Antonio's best friend, Jesse, and his girlfriend, Jill, live in Cleveland, Ohio. I crashed on their floor last night, and they are joining me on the road today to shoot some photos for people following the ride online.

The terrain has flattened out, but the headwinds are still brutal, and the sky is crowded with metal-gray clouds. It's like pedaling on a treadmill, having to fight for every mile.

"This isn't working. I'll never get anywhere like this." My voice is shaky with frustration when I find Jesse and Jill waiting by the side of the road. "I have to change direction somehow. Even the wind at an angle would be better."

Jesse pulls out a map, and we plan a series of roads that zigzag south and northwest to avoid direct headwinds.

At least the terrain is flat, and I manage to pick up some speed over the next few hours. I spot my friends' car parked up a side road just as Jill gets out and waves me down. Swerving sharply to make the turn in time, Pegasus's wheels slip on the gravel surface, and we skid a few yards. I lie still, slightly dazed, arms spread like a crucified Christ. I let my head drop back and stare up at the sky. "Huh. Gravel works exactly like black ice. Who knew?"

"Oh my God!" shouts Jesse as he races over, mouth open, hands flailing wildly around his head.

I realize he can't see my eyes behind the dark glasses and

must think I'm out cold. This appeals to my dark sense of humor, so I continue to lie unmoving to watch his reaction.

Jill runs over as Jesse really starts to panic. "Oh my God. She's not moving! What do we do?"

I let them squirm a little longer, till phrases like "911" and "call an ambulance" tell me it's probably time to end the mischief.

"I'm *fine*, Jesse," I jump up, laughing.

"Juliana! I—I can't believe you!" he sputters. "That is a terrible joke! How could you do that?"

"Sorry, but your reaction was priceless. I couldn't *not* do it. *"Oh my God! Oh my God!"* I mimic his head-in-hands panic.

"You did look pretty funny," Jill agrees.

Finally he laughs, probably more from relief than because he finds it remotely amusing.

The skin down my thigh has been flayed, and it's burning, blood seeping through my cycling shorts and torn shirt-sleeve, but the sun breaks through the clouds as I enter Defiance County. The name seems appropriate. Today I'm determined not to be beaten. My target is to reach the small town of Hicksville, a few miles from the border of Ohio and Indiana. Jesse and Jill drive on ahead to find a motel for the night.

Motels in these tiny towns are basic and utilitarian, but finding a place to stay is never a problem. The trouble is finding somewhere to *eat* after eight p.m. I usually pedal till sundown, rarely stopping earlier than eight-thirty, but nobody seems to eat late in middle America. Restaurants and diners are often closed by the time I have found a place to stay and gone in search of food.

It is already dark when Jesse and Jill find me on the road, still a few miles outside Hicksville. Despite the tumble, I pedaled 133 miles today, and I'm feeling pretty pleased with myself.

The motel we check into is run by a grumpy old woman who huffs and puffs her way around her unresponsive husband, filling out the registration forms and then ordering him to escort me to my room.

"Now, there's a life-size painting of a man on your wall. Supposed to be a theme from some famous novel. Don't let it startle you. It was there when we took the place over," she hollers at me as I follow her silent spouse to a smaller building behind the main one.

The guest in the room next door to mine is tall, with gray hair and stubble across his face, wearing a blue-collared shirt tucked into jeans. He watches me wheel Pegasus up to the door, clearly looking for an opening to make conversation.

"Hi! I'm yer neighbor," he says.

I smile, nod, and carry my bike inside the room. The "man on the wall" is resplendent in an old captain's hat and dark blue jacket, smoking a pipe, with the sea and a lighthouse behind him. He could be *Moby-Dick*'s Captain Ahab or Santiago from *The Old Man and the Sea*, I can't decide which. The entire room is decorated in an ocean theme.

I wash my cycling clothes and hang them over any available furniture, hoping they'll dry by tomorrow. My friendly neighbor is still loitering as I leave the room to go for dinner with Jesse and Jill.

"How tall are ya?" is his next stab at conversation.

"I don't know," I answer, feeling uncomfortable when he falls into step directly behind me.

"Cuz, yer real tall, y'know?"

"I know."

"I seen ya with a bike."

"Yup." I stop in front of Jesse and Jill's room and knock.

"Where ya headed?" He is standing too close for comfort now, his face right in mine.

"Across America, to Seattle."

"Ah, didn't nobody tell ya? Yer goin' the wrong way!" He guffaws.

"Yes. You are certainly not the first to mention it."

"See ya later!" he hollers as Jesse and Jill open the door, and I'm pretty sure he means it.

The only place open, and possibly serving food, is a little dive bar a couple of miles down the road.

"Do you think Hicksville was named after its people, or do the people live up to the name?" Jill asks as we watch the colorful local nightlife around us.

A couple of wannabe hiphop hicks are sitting at the bar across from our table. The more vociferous of the two is a gangly youth dressed in an oversize T-shirt, with a gaudy silver chain around his neck, backward cap over his cropped ginger hair, and minuscule headphones around his neck. One hand clapped on the shoulder of his chubby companion, he shouts across the bar, "Hey, Carly! Earlie here's won himself a six-pack! Carly! Earlie's sharin' his six-pack! Get yo' ass over here!"

Carly shows signs of having downed a great many six-packs already today. He has one arm thrown around a three-foot tall blond woman eating French fries and the other around a leathery-skinned woman who looks sixty but is probably forty. "My favorite ladies! Give us a kiss!" he roars, swooping down to plant one on the blonde's cheek, while she ducks nimbly away. The older woman rolls her eyes and chuckles, "Sure we are. You only say that after you've had too many."

"Carly!" Bucktooth shouts again. "Leave them ladies and get yo' ass over here if you want a beer!"

More giggles from Earlie. Carly stomps expectantly over, crushing each teenager affectionately under a sweaty armpit.

"Beer!" he shouts at the bar girl, a wiry tomboy in a T-shirt and ripped jeans. "Let's have it then! Where's that six-pack?"

"Hold yer horses." She scowls at him, evidently used to handling boisterous regulars. She opens the fridge and plonks a pack of Bud Light onto the bar.

Our orders arrive as the excitement starts to escalate. We eat quickly, but not as quickly as the six-pack is downed. The locals are getting rowdy. "It's probably a good idea to go," Jesse says. "In a few more minutes bottles will start breaking."

He and Jill escort me to my bedroom door, where, as promised, my neighbor is waiting.

"What's your sun sign?" he greets me.

"I don't know." I opt for evasion, quickly inserting the key and opening the door.

He notices Jesse hovering nearby. "Where you folks from?"

"Cleveland. Just accompanying Juliana here for some of the road."

"That's awful nice of you."

"Yeah, it's been fun." Jesse keeps my neighbor distracted while I retreat into the room.

"'Night, guys." I close the door as Jesse gives me a thumbs-up. I can hear the guy trying to make small talk, Jesse saying something about having to go to bed, the crunch of gravel as he walks away.

After brushing my teeth and turning out the lights, I hear the unmistakable sound of the door handle turning back and forth. Or maybe I've just watched too many hostel horror films. Either way, I get up and check that the door is double locked and bolted before going to sleep.

AUGUST 12, 2012

Jesse and Jill left me in Indiana yesterday and drove back to Cleveland, and now I have stopped in Rochester to try to fix the gears, which are still jumping. There are no bike mechanics around, except for an enthusiastic amateur named Dennis, who works out of the garage at the back of his house, helping friends and neighbors with minor repairs. Like the mechanics who've already looked at it, he's unable to fix the shifter problem, but he does change my tires over a couple of cold beers. Then he and his wife take me out for an Italian dinner. The mushy pasta smothered in processed cheese is awful, but the company is wonderful.

The generosity and open-natured kindness of the Americans I have met continue to impress me. Unlike the Europeans, with their ancient cultures, who can behave like cynical old-timers who have seen it all and are hard to impress, many of the people I encounter in America still seem to embody the curiosity and openness of a young, fledgling country. They are less prone to sarcasm and pretense. A stranger cycling through is a natural curiosity. Anytime I stop on the road, within minutes someone will pull up to assist, chat, or even invite me to their home for dinner.

This afternoon, having pulled off the road to take a call from Antonio, hunched over the handlebars to speak into my phone, two women stop their cars to ask if I am okay. I have never experienced this level of camaraderie anywhere. "That's just us Americans," one of them tells me. "You'll never stay in trouble long here."

Whenever I pass someone, I always receive a wave, an observation, or a piece of advice. Like the woman driving a lawn mower over the sprawling green turf behind her country home. I had been pedaling up and down a roller-coaster road on what felt like an endless series of hills. She stopped to watch as I crested another hill, waiting till I cruised by on the way down, to holler, "It doesn't get any better! Them hills go on like that forever!"

I'm in Illinois, heading toward Peoria, and it has not stopped raining since I crossed the state line. My shoes are drenched, my feet are numb, and only the audiobook in my earphones distracts from the utter physical misery. I decided on American authors for the ride across the States, and Philip Roth's novella *The Dying Animal* is the current choice on my playlist.

Since I stopped early yesterday, having covered only ninety miles, I plan to make up the lost ground today, despite the rain. It could be worse. There could be headwinds.

"Let's get it done," I tell Pegasus, which is exactly what we are doing when, speeding down an incline, I clock the railroad tracks too late. The earth around the rails has caved away, leaving deep ruts full of water. I have no choice but to brake and swerve at the last moment. That second before impact is one of the longest on earth. Everything slows down, but at the same time it all happens so quickly that you don't have time to register any of it until it's over.

I hit the ground hard this time, with one foot still attached to the pedal. My helmet saves my head, bouncing against the tracks like a basketball. My left arm hurts when I flex it, my wrist feels sprained, and blood is seeping through my shorts.

Now both thighs are badly bruised and flayed. On the bright side, at least I will have matching scars.

Bits and pieces have flown off the bike, and there are fresh gashes in the white paint, but overall Pegasus suffered less damage than me. Shaken, I put the bike back together, realign the chain, and sit down on the tarmac to settle my nerves. *Note to self: in future, watch out for train tracks.*

Equilibrium restored, I climb back onto the bike, determined not to let the fall break my stride. I pedal painfully on through the interminable drizzle, Philip Roth in my ears reminding me that "like all enjoyable things, you see, it has unenjoyable parts to it."

AUGUST 14, 2012

Larger towns and cities mean a potential Starbucks, which means finding a passable coffee. Since leaving Italy, my search for good espresso has become a daily preoccupation. It's almost silly how the everyday little things in life take on such disproportionate importance when you find yourself without them.

Google Maps has revealed that there is a Starbucks in Peoria, so I decide to stop there for lunch. I'm just parking Pegasus against the wall when I hear someone shouting my name. A blond woman in shorts and a T-shirt is stepping out of a black Jeep holding a fluorescent green sign that reads, GO JULIANA!

"Are you Juliana?" she asks, coming over.

"Er, yes?"

"We've been expecting you to pass by. I'm Marsha. My son and I have been following your progress on the Spot tracker since we heard about your ride from a friend. We wanted to put you up for the night, but I guess the timing's off. I thought I'd meet you on the road anyway and give you some snacks." She hands me a plastic bag full of energy bars and chocolate. Happy days. "Are you stopping for lunch?"

"Yes, just this minute actually."

"What a crazy coincidence! I was just about to drive out to find you along the road when you pulled up here right in front of me. I can't believe my luck. Let me offer you lunch."

We eat Subway sandwiches, and I tell her all about my adventures across America so far, including the bike trouble I've been having.

"You know my son, Bradley, worked part time for a bike shop here called Bushwackers. They can fix just about anything."

"That would be brilliant if they can repair my bike. The last two places told me I'd have to change the shifter, but if it can be fixed, that would save me a lot of money." At least six hundred dollars.

"Sure, I can take you there now if you want. Bradley wanted to meet you, too. I'll let him know where we are."

"Thank you!"

"It's the least I can do. Sorry we can't put you up for the night." She dials a number and speaks to someone from the bike shop. Hanging up, she says, "Okay, the mechanic is in, and he seems optimistic he can fix the problem."

Bushwackers turns out to be a huge outdoors store, a large section of which is devoted to cycling. In the back is a workshop where the bike mechanic, Gary, is waiting. His wavy hair is gray, and he has the wiry physique of a longtime cyclist.

"Let's have a look at it." He takes Pegasus off my hands, secures it on to the repair stand, turns the pedals, shifts the gears, checks the slack on the cable, and shakes his head. "Who tightened this? It's *waaay* too tight."

"The last mechanic I took it to. Thought that might be the problem. He didn't know much about this kind of shifter."

"He just made it worse. Don't have to change the part, though. Can fix this easily."

Finally a mechanic who knows what he is doing! While he works, I check out the store's selection of reinforced tires. I am sick and tired of changing tubes, and a new pair of tires is long overdue. I'm out of the workshop only about five minutes, but Gary has already finished by the time I get back.

"Problem solved," he says matter-of-factly.

"*Already?*" I'm impressed. "Do you think I might get the tires changed while you've got Pegasus up there?"

"Don't see why not."

Pegasus has a brand-new set of rubber in under five minutes.

"Can I take you with me?" I ask.

"I would love that. The wife might be less enthusiastic, though."

Thinking this day couldn't get any better, the shop owner

gives me a discount on the tires. Then he says, "We won't charge you for the work, either."

It all comes to a fraction of what I would have had to pay for a new shifter. Thank God for road angels.

AUGUST 15–16, 2012

After crossing the MacArthur Bridge over the Mississippi river into Iowa, I pull off at a service station to use the toilet and stock up on water. Waiting in line at the counter with some protein bars and a couple of bottles, I can't help overhearing the conversation between the cashier and a local customer.

"Yup, they're drivin' around town with an AK-47 and a BB gun, shootin' up people's cars, people's dawgs, people's windows." An acute reminder that America, "the land of the free," is also the land of the "free to carry weapons." I decide discretion is the better part of valor and hightail it out of town as fast as I can pedal.

My route passes through the drift plains of southern Iowa. The gently rolling hills, carpeted in the standard agricultural staples of wheat and corn, make for easy, if monotonous, pedaling. Give me a tailwind—or no wind—and I should reach Missouri within a couple of days.

AUGUST 18, 2012

Zigzagging through country roads on a detour through a tiny town, somewhere in east Missouri, population under two hundred, the tarmac suddenly ends. I find myself on an unpaved road, with the main state highway some five miles away, according to the GPS. Pegasus wobbles and bumps against the large, jagged gravel, and eventually I'm forced to dismount and walk. The GPS is struggling to get a reading now, leading me down a maze of stony paths. The miles stretch on and on, and the GPS keeps replotting the route for roads that don't exist. It's exasperating.

"Stupid fucking satnav. Stupid fucking roads." *Under certain circumstances, profanity provides a relief denied even to prayer,* said the veteran adventurer Mark Twain, who clearly knew all about it. The road continues as far as I can see in either direction. Trekking under the sweltering sun, hungry and out of water, my mood starts to plummet as dehydration, hunger, and irritation rise. An old farm jalopy hurtles down the road toward me, kicking up clouds of white dust. I put out my hand, and the gnarly, graying driver in jean overalls slows up next to me.

"Excuse me, could you tell me if this is the right direction for the state highway?"

"Yup, I guess. But you got at least another three miles. Ain't a good road for that bike." He spits out a mouthful of brown tobacco juice.

"No shit." Few things annoy me like people who state the obvious.

After an hour's walking I finally get back on tarmac. My throat feels like the gravel road I have just been down. The next town is a few miles farther on, and I stop inside the first Subway I find. The sandwich chain has been sustaining me throughout America as it's slightly healthier than the other fast-food options and it has branches almost everywhere. I order a foot-long sandwich and Gatorade from the woman on the other side of the counter. She gives me a sidelong glance and raises a single eyebrow.

I must be a sooty sight. I can feel the grit and dust sticking to my sweat. I am trying to forget what "bathed and clean" feels like, forget smelling good, and most of all, forget dignity. I slink off to the toilet in the hope of washing some of the grime from my face and arms. It is not much better when I have finished, but it will have to do. Stuffing down the roast beef and avocado sandwich helps raise my mood a few levels closer to normal.

AUGUST 19, 2012

I have hit Nebraska, where even Subways are hard to find. Decent food is a rare treat here. I am in wilderness country now. Nothing for miles between tiny deserted towns consisting of a few neglected shacks and houses, each with a population under ninety. The plains stretch into infinity. It is easy to imagine oneself back in the Wild West, where Comanches on horseback hunted wild buffalo. The terrain is flat, and for the first time in America, I have a powerful tailwind. In addition, I gain an extra hour of daylight when I cross the time zone.

"Let's get it done," I tell Pegasus again. It is a good day to push hard, and we cover 170 miles. Days like this one remind me of just how much ground I could be covering were I going in the opposite direction, with consistent tailwinds. Thinking about it gets depressing.

Most days blend into each other on the road. Days without incident. The impression of moving while time hangs in suspension. Long hours of sitting in the saddle, punctuated only by brief stops for food and water. These short breaks become the highlights of my day. I can muse for hours over what I will eat or drink when next I stop. What will I treat myself to after fifty miles? Will I have a Coke, a Red Bull, or a coffee? Shall I try that new peanut butter chocolate bar or some beef jerky?

A woman at a service station informs me there have been massive forest fires sweeping through the north of Wyoming. Seeing Yellowstone National Park has always been high on my wish list, and I've been looking forward to pedaling through it, so the news is disappointing. I will have to take a route passing through the south of Wyoming instead. One of the essential skills I'm cultivating on the road is flexibility. Anything can happen, and when it does, you have to adapt. Where there is a problem, there is always a solution.

I have stopped for lunch in the tiny border town of Pine Bluffs, just after crossing from Nebraska into Wyoming. It has the crumbling, derelict appearance of a ghost town. There are a few shops and diners with broken windows and boarded-up doors. The only place that seems to be open is a dive bar called Pal's pub, where I hope to find at least a hamburger and fries.

It is a dimly lit, smoky joint with neon signs, old caps, saddles, pictures, and random paraphernalia covering the walls. A line of similarly overweight, bearded locals wearing cowboy hats, checked shirts, and colorful suspenders are sitting along the length of the bar. The cowboys give me a brief once-over before unanimously turning back to their beers.

"Do you serve food?" I ask the aging female bartender. The deep lines creasing her face are downturned in a permanent scowl. I imagine she has been here her entire life, stubbornly refusing to go anywhere else, while her neighbors have shut down and boarded up their businesses and the little town has slowly faded into oblivion. I wonder whether Pine Bluffs will become one more abandoned middle-American town within a few years.

"Read the board," she snaps back, signaling with her thumb to a blackboard behind the bar.

It's difficult to make out the faint white chalk scribblings in the neon-blue bar light. chicken burger and chips, $4, reads the only item on the menu.

"Guess I'll have the chicken burger and chips."

"What're ya drinkin'?"

"A Coke, please."

I sit at one of the dark wooden tables, and she plunks a warm Coke can down in front of me. Too intimidated to ask for a glass and ice, I watch as she stomps back over to the bar, pulls a box out of a freezer, tears it open, and tosses something inside the microwave. Five minutes later she's back, carrying a plastic plate with the "burger"—a defrosted, breaded chicken patty the consistency of rubber—sandwiched between a dry white bun that tastes of chemicals, with a bag of plain potato chips on the side. To think I have been looking forward to *this* all day! Hungry as I am, I cannot eat the burger, so I swallow my stinging disappointment along with the chips and leave my four dollars on the table.

I am fully aware of how absurd it is that something as basic as food has the ability to affect my mood. I usually try to keep things light; it's always easier to deal with little problems or difficult people with humor. But when I'm hungry, I can quickly become snappy, capricious, and grumpy. When life is stripped down and minimized to the absolute essentials, then silly things like the quality of food can get blown out of all proportion. To keep my negative emotions in check, I go into deep energy-conservation mode. This means *keep still, keep quiet, keep calm.*

Keep everything in perspective, I tell myself. I think about what food was like as a child growing up in develop-

ing countries across Asia and Africa. Almost nothing was
eaten for pleasure. It was all just fuel, plain and awful. Fruit
and vegetables were scavenged from the bins behind market
stalls. It took hours to cut out the "good bits" from the rot-
ten. Then everything was boiled until it was tasteless. As
staples, beans and lentils came second only to livers and
hearts, the cheapest protein anywhere in the world. If we
were hungry, we filled up on rice. I remember thinking the
impoverished locals ate better than we did. Food portions
were rationed out, and we ate every last thing set before us,
giving thanks, asking no questions, because beggars can't be
choosers, and we were "beggars for Christ," or "missionaries," as the adults preferred to call themselves. When I grew
up, I swore I would never willingly eat "bad" food again.
Now I chuckle to think how I wouldn't mind some plain
boiled beans and rice at this moment, and how "good" and
"bad" are entirely relative and circumstantial terms.

I get back on my bike and start pedaling up the road
when I happen upon a deli. Salvation! How can I describe
my elation in this moment? Compared to the inedible dive-
bar burger, the deli steak and cheese sandwich tastes like
Michelin-star cuisine. If I have learned nothing else thus far,
I have learned how to appreciate the little things—and what
is existence except a giant conglomeration of little things?
We don't even realize our reliance on them, how much we
take them for granted, until we are without them. Even
essentials like food and water. It takes loss and privation for
us to discover the true value of something or someone. This
is the strange nature of humans.

A FERRY TALE

The flat, desolate wilderness of Nebraska has continued through the south of Wyoming, but with an awe-inspiring variation. Mammoth rock formations cut through the landscape, rising out of the silver and green sagebrush like ancient petrified titans. This country takes my breath away. It is a country for gods, animals, and philosophers.

I have been meeting a lot of Harley bikers and their leather-clad ladies at the service station rest stops along the highway. "We were heading north, passing through Yellowstone Park, and had to detour south because of the fires," one couple tells me. "Don't be headin' north, whatever you do. We just come from there. The roads are impassable."

Once again I am relieved to have gotten wind of the fires ahead of time and preemptively shifted my route south.

The bikers give me a salute and shout something I can't hear over their revving motors as they roar out of the station. This country is ideal for social rebels. It certainly touches something archaic and primitive in me. I feel like a cowgirl heading west on my white stallion. Civilization seems very far away and very futile. A girl could happily disappear into the wilds here. I have fantasies of building a rough log cabin somewhere in the middle of the sagebrush-covered hills and dropping off the radar entirely.

It has been a month since I set off from Naples, but the time feels much longer and much shorter than that, as though I have always traveled like this, and always could, forever.

AUGUST 26, 2012

Mark Webber is a photographer who specializes in shooting outdoor adventurers. He heard about my journey through a mutual friend and has now met me in Twin Falls, Idaho, to follow me on the road for an afternoon and take some photos. Rain is threatening, but the wind is at my back, and I am flying past some incredible scenery on the Thousand Springs Scenic Byway. Cascades of spring water jettison out of the winding, phosphorous cliffs of Snake River Canyon. Two storms are rushing in behind me from the northeast and the southeast, and the force of the two winds acts as a powerful propellant. I pedal with a ridiculous grin stretching my cheeks.

Antonio calls. "What's going on?"

"What do you mean?"

"The tracker says you're averaging twenty-two miles an hour."

"Is that all? It feels much faster."

"So it's correct?"

"Better believe it! *Woohoo!*"

It feels like I have won the lottery. If I could have this kind of wind every day, I would make it around the world in eighty days. I would have finished the United States long ago. The contrast reminds me once again of just how much the almost constant headwinds have impeded my progress across North America.

Mark is somewhere nearby, snapping photos. He's been pulling his truck off the road and scrambling up cliff faces to get aerial shots of me and Pegasus racing by. I catch no more than flashes of him every so often, waiting by the side of the road. When he isn't photographing adventures, Mark is a professional rock climber. He combines the best of both his talents to produce some incredible shots.

Eventually the two storms catch up and break over us in a clash of thunder and icy sheets of rain, so I pull over at a roadside bar. It is only midafternoon, but I have already covered nearly 125 miles. I feel like kicking back.

"Let's have a beer," I suggest to Mark.

"You want to drink *now*?"

"Why not? This rain's gonna go on for at least another hour."

We sit quietly at the bar and drink our beers, but I feel like dancing a merry jig on the bar top. The mood I'm in, I am up for just about anything. There have been bad days, but this is definitely not one of them. When the storm eventually blows itself out and the sun breaks through, Mark wishes me luck and heads home. Meanwhile I continue for another fifteen miles and stop for the night in Glenns Ferry, Idaho.

AUGUST 27, 2012

I grab breakfast—some banana bread, yogurt, and a carton of milky coffee—in a supermarket and eat it in the park across the road. By the time I come back to the typical forty-dollar-a-night motel—you know the kind: beige carpets and garishly patterned bedcover and drapes—to pay the bill, the manager is in his office. While he putters around, searching for the receipt book, I check out the black-and-white photo display on the wall depicting Glenns Ferry in various stages of its history.

"How old is this town?" I ask.

"How old is this town? Well . . ." The question seems to stump him momentarily. He strokes the stubble on his chin, scratches his balding scalp, and asks, "Where are you from?"

"Italy."

"Italy, huh." His eyes dart from side to side, and he appears to be making some sort of mental calculation. He finally comes back with: "Well, back when the world began—"

I start to laugh, but from the look on his face, I realize he's not kidding and swallow my smile.

"—the first humans came over in ships."

"You mean the early settlers?" I interject, trying to help.

"Yep, them settlers. And they started making their way west, following the Oregon Trail, which passes through here. Now, there is this river they had to cross, and on this river was this ferry. And this guy called Glenn used to take the settlers over the river on the ferry."

Apparently the river, ferry, and Glenn were already magically there, back when the world began.

"Ah, so that's why the town is called Glenns Ferry."

He nods. "So I guess you could say it dates from . . . hmmm . . . somewhere back in the 1800s."

From this brief history lesson I learn that both time and history are fluid.

AUGUST 28, 2012

The route I have planned passes through Baker City, Oregon, heads north toward Yakima, and then cuts across to Seattle, where I plan to catch a flight to New Zealand. There are a few long climbs, but nothing as painful as the mountains in Portugal, nor half as verdant and lush. It is late August in the northern Rockies, and the dry summers are getting drier all the time, so the arid landscape doesn't vary much between various shades of brown and ochre. Halfway up a climb near the Idaho-Oregon border, I get my ninth puncture and pull off to the side of the highway to change the tube.

A few miles farther, throat parched from the heat and

dust kicked up by passing trucks, I stop at a service station to fill up on water. A Range Rover drives up as I'm sitting on the step, munching on a chocolate peanut butter bar, and a group of Californians pile out, all chattering at full volume: "I mean, back in LA, we never see this kind of wilderness and desolation. I couldn't believe we hardly saw a single tree passing through Wyoming. What an incredible drive. Real challenging."

One of the women, with dyed-blond hair in an exaggerated perm and giant sunglasses, notices me and Pegasus leaned up against the wall. "Where're you cyclin' from, honey?" she asks.

"Boston to Seattle."

Her mouth drops open, and she elbows one of her companions. "You believe that? She's pedaled from Boston!"

"No kidding. We drove over from New York, and I thought *that* was difficult enough," her friend says.

The day's difficulties are not quite over. The service station manager informs me that the longest uphill stretch still lies ahead. "You're gonna climb for a while. Let me tell you, I wouldn't want to be you. No sirrreeee." She shakes her head.

"There are times when I wouldn't want to be me either," I admit.

Somewhere along that seemingly endless uphill road, I feel myself floating, as in a lucid dream, my limbs mechanically pumping, but I can't really feel them. Maybe I've been pedaling under the sun for too long. The passage of time seems indefinite, transient. I have one of those moments when I wonder if any of it is real. I grab the flesh on my arm and squeeze it hard to assure myself that it is, but even the knowledge that pinching my skin is meant to generate pain tells my brain it must be so. I start to wonder, if the mind can create any reality it chooses, then what is truly real? Maybe our bodies are just machines and life is a game we are all hooked into. Maybe reality is what is not "here," is not what we think is "us."

I know that my body is tired, hungry, and fatigued, yet I keep pushing on, and eventually the moment of self-punishment becomes pure inner expansion. If our minds can surpass the dictates of our bodies, then surely we are capable of anything. Everything starts in the mind. That is the seat of power, of whether we succeed or fail, of the beginning and the end of it all. When the mind gives up, the body soon follows.

I push my protesting muscles up the hill, and I'm rewarded with a red sun setting against a vivid vermilion sky, jutting ridges of rock to my left, and the river snaking along to the right. I stand up on the pedals, Wagner blaring through my earphones, the fresh wind against my skin, a giant grin on my face and miles of pure downhill bliss ahead of me. It is the rush of feeling connected to everything, to life itself. A microcosm of a universal macrocosm. I feel 100 percent alive. Nothing else exists except for this perfect moment.

And suddenly I am weeping for no apparent reason. Fatigue, stress, exhaustion, happiness, exhilaration? Life is a strange thing. You can create a reality to make it all easier to bear, then discover that you love the world you've created and it takes on a life of its own. Maybe none of this is real? Perhaps it is all just a ride? We forget who we are, and these moments awaken something in us that makes us remember we are the creators of our own worlds, our thoughts, our emotions.

Hendri believed the purpose of existence was to express our consciousness and thereby to create our universe.

Juliana: Do you believe there must be a purpose for existence?

Hendri: Next level . . . Think there is . . . reason . . . not sure.

Juliana: Tell me why you think so.

Hendri: Perhaps existence is enough. But there are levels of that.

Juliana: In my opinion mere "existence" is overrated.

Hendri: I heard a good one recently: our reason for existence is to express our consciousness.

Juliana: Why "express our consciousness"? Who does it profit?

Hendri: That is a good point. Let's get back to that as soon as you answer why you think existence is overrated.

Juliana: Just to "exist" puts you at the same level as animals. In essence, that's what existence is: eating, shitting, sleeping. So what defines mankind as above animals?

Hendri: But we can express consciousness. That puts us far above animals. We can create the universe

through our perceptions, our thoughts. You have
to admit, that's pretty cool.

I get it now, Hendri.

AUGUST 30, 2012

In my last push toward Seattle, I decide to take the interstate
highway. This is not recommended and possibly even illegal.
Looking on Google Maps, there are alternatives, but they all
mean cycling a more mountainous route that will take longer, and I'm on a tight deadline. As I did with the flight out
of Europe, I've bought my airline ticket a couple of days in
advance, so I have to reach the airport by that date.

Even with reinforced tires, the amount of litter on the
interstate means inevitable punctures. In addition, my bike
has been fitted with carbon spoke nipples instead of the
cheaper but more durable steel. Fine for racing, not so good
for cycling the world. Two of the nipples snap off, so I screw
down the spokes as a temporary solution until I can find a
bike shop. The front wheel is wobbling alarmingly, and every
time I hit a bump, I worry that the uneven pressure will cause
further damage. By the time I reach Seattle, Pegasus has suffered ten punctures and three broken spoke nipples.

A friend who was born and raised in the Moonies—
otherwise known as the Unification Church, another infamous cult that gained popularity in the sixties and
seventies—has offered to put me up in Seattle. I first met

Donna a couple of years ago in London, when we gave a presentation together at a conference about the challenges ex-cult kids face when trying to integrate into society. As the first "blessed" child born into the Moonies in the Western world, she grew up, as I did, mostly without her parents. Instead, she was entrusted to the care of random members of the group in a succession of "boarding schools." Like me, she began to question her situation from a young age and was immediately labeled a rebel. Like me, she led a double life within the group until she made the transition into mainstream society. And like me, she became vocal about the lack of rights for children growing up within cults, for which the Moonies demonized her.

It is late by the time I arrive at Donna's house, and she's waiting outside as I roll up. She is a striking blonde with blue eyes and the kind of ready smile that makes you think of chocolate chip cookies and warm milk. Before long I have taken advantage of her giant bath to indulge in a long soak. The hot soapy water is bliss. When I emerge after an hour, I could swear my skin is a couple of shades lighter. The water, in any case, is definitely several shades darker.

AUGUST 31, 2012

Donna has accompanied me to a nearby bike shop this morning, so the mechanics can give Pegasus a thorough clean, change the broken nipples and chain, and fit new reinforced tires. It's late by the time I start cycling to the airport, and I'm in a race against the clock as I pedal the last twenty miles to the departures terminal. Once there I'll still have to disassemble and box Pegasus for the flight, which will take a good half hour.

The road is lined with stoplights the entire way, which slows progress considerably. I'm keeping time with an orange city bus, starting and stopping together at the lights. A group of young guys get off at one stop, then wait at the zebra crossing for the pedestrian signal to turn green. One of them—an African American with dreadlocks—keeps glancing over in my direction as if he's busting to say something. Unable to contain himself, he finally blurts out, "You know, that bus driver was checkin' out yo' booty!"

"Can't say I blame him," I fire back. "I'd probably do the same."

He looks around to make sure his buddies are clocking his pluck. "Oh yeah? Well, in that case, so was I!" He doubles over with laughter, one fist jammed to his mouth. At that moment the green pedestrian signal blinks on, and he skips lightly across the road, high-fiving his friends like he's just sneaked a cookie from the jar.

I make it to the airport just in time to box the bike and board the plane, then sleep the whole fifteen-hour flight to New Zealand. Except, of course, when they come around with food. For the first time ever, I clean every little plastic dish on the dinner tray and ask for another, if they have any to spare. The flight attendant clearly understands what is expected of her the next time around. My breakfast tray comes laden with two of everything.

RAINBOWS, HOBBITS, AND HEADWINDS

SEPTEMBER 5, 2012

New Zealand is the land of rainbows. I've never seen so many, so frequently, except perhaps in Ireland. Both countries share another thing, too: it has been raining off and on like a leaky faucet ever since I landed in Auckland. Then there are the winds. Apparently New Zealand is also known for its gale-force winds. None of this is entirely consistent with the romantic images I conjured of my journey through the set of Tolkien's fantasy land in the *Lord of the Rings* blockbuster trilogy. I've wanted to visit the country ever since watching the films, so I was thrilled when it turned out to be one of the few options I had when it came to choosing antipodal points I had to touch on my route.

After hitting Hamilton, one of the larger cities directly south of Auckland, my GPS suddenly stops working, my smartphone battery dies, and I'm unable to find a shop that sells maps. As there are next to no signs out in the countryside, find-ing my way becomes a lot of guesswork and asking for direc-tions. Either I don't understand the locals or they don't understand me, because somewhere along the way I get on the wrong road. I was intending to head for Te Kuiti and follow the west coast all the way to Wellington, but now I'm someplace in the middle of the North Island, surrounded by rolling hills.

"Where are you?" Antonio asks when he finally manages to contact me on the emergency phone. It's three a.m. in Italy. He's been waking up every hour to check if my tracker has moved and to try to reach me by phone.

"I don't know. The locals keep pointing me in all kinds of directions."

"Well, where's the last place you passed?"

"Can't you see where I am on the tracker?"

"No. It hasn't updated since yesterday. I thought some-thing must have happened to you."

Sure enough, my Spot tracker is blinking red. I have no idea what this means, except that green is good, so red must be bad.

"You're right. It doesn't seem to be working."

"Is it the batteries?"

"I don't think so. I changed them in the States. Anyway, I don't have any spares, if that's the problem."

"Fuck. That's bad. What do we do if I can't see where you are and can't contact you? It's impossible to help you if I don't know where you are."

"I just passed a small town called Tokoroa."

"One moment." Antonio goes online to check my loca-tion. "Ju—what the fuck? You're near Lake Taupo, right in the middle. You are heading straight for the worst mountains. You were supposed to follow the coast!" He's shouting into the phone like a good southern Italian. This always makes me nervous. The one thing about living in southern Italy that I will never get used to is the shouting. The constant noise. The stress-inducing, over-the-top drama that is normal life to a Mediterranean native.

I remember the first time Antonio invited me to his family's home for lunch. In Naples, Sunday lunch is an indispensable tradition. The mamma spends the entire morning cooking at least three courses, which the whole family then proceeds to inhale within a few short minutes. I quickly learned to scarf down my food if I wanted to get a full meal. (Eating fast—another useful road skill.) Antonio's father, mother, and brother were all shouting at the top of their lungs, with his mother, Anna Maria, the loudest of them all. Her voice punctuated the others' sentences like sharp exclamation points. I thought I had stepped into a family feud.

"What are they arguing about?" I whispered to Antonio.

"*Arguing?* Cute!" He laughed and pinched my cheek. "They're discussing the recipe for the stuffed eggplant."

"*Buono?*" Anna Maria asked me just then, her voice like an explosion of thunder out of industrial speakers, so loud that I did a startled little jump. Everybody saw it. The room went quiet for about three seconds, then they all broke into peals of laughter.

"My grandmother was deaf," Antonio explained. "Mamma got used to shouting. Maybe it's why we're all a little deaf, too."

For Antonio, his family, and every good Neapolitan, speaking normally equates to what anyone else would consider shouting. This also means that their shouting comes close to eardrum-tearing decibels. So over the phone right now, Antonio's voice raises my stress levels to the breaking point. I fire back at a volume I think he will understand: "Yes, Antonio! I *would* be following the coast, except I have no maps, no GPS, and there are no bloody signs!"

"Why are you shouting?" he asks. I do it so rarely, the novelty always unsettles him.

"I'm shouting because *you* are shouting, and I'm stressed enough as it is."

"I don't know what to tell you. You're completely fucked."

Antonio's blunt assessment of the situation does not help my pissy mood. "Thanks. Real helpful. What do you suggest I do?"

"Turn around."

"I can't. Not allowed. Guinness World Record rules state you cannot go backward during the attempt."

"Then you really are fucked."

"Oh, for God's sake, would you stop that?"

"There's only one other town near you. It's called Mangakino. I suggest you stop there for the day and replan your route. Any direction you go now, you'll have to cross very bad mountains."

It is already midafternoon and I have not eaten since breakfast. I am feeling weak and dizzy, my body has the shakes, and my throat is sore, probably the onset of a cold from the wind and rain. To make matters worse, my period has just started, and the first day is always the worst for cramps. I decide to head for Mangakino, eat something, charge my phone, and buy a map, if I can find one.

Antonio isn't finished with the bad news, though. "By the way, Ju. The money for the attempt is finished. You have just three hundred euros left in the account. If nothing arrives in the next couple of days, you'll have to come home. Actually I don't even know how you'll come home. There isn't enough money for a ticket."

I am hitting a record low now. I am too tired to think. What I need is a long sleep. Morning usually brings clarity, so tomorrow I'll regroup and come up with a plan. I pedal to Mangakino, where I decide to call it a day.

The town reminds me of one of those depressing mining settlements composed primarily of dingy prefab housing. There is a hostel near the river undergoing refurbishment, but they agree to give me a bed for the night. Just as I'm thinking my luck has changed, my hopes drop again when the young English blonde in charge tells me the Internet is down, and no, they don't have any paper maps of New Zealand.

How will I plan my route for tomorrow? My dejection is tangible. It's been one of those one-thing-after-another kind of days. I meander down a narrow dirt path leading to the river to have a think. There is a little makeshift bar on the bank, run by an elderly gentleman who offers me a drink. In the summer, his establishment also serves food to tourists and locals engaged in water sports on the river. He is experimenting with making pizza for the upcoming season's customers, while his English friend, who is sitting across the

table from me, is sampling his culinary creations. I am cor-
dially invited to join them.

Contrary to what many people believe, more topping on
a pizza does not mean better. The Neapolitans, who invented
the dish, are truly minimalist: it's always a case of quality
ingredients over quantity. Most will ever eat only the original pizza, with tomato, mozzarella, and basil. The taste is
exquisite. If you have to throw a bunch of crap on top, by
their reasoning, the pizza is probably not very good in the
first place. What's more, placing frozen, mixed Asian stir-
fry vegetables on a pizza would be considered a comestible
travesty. Any native of Naples would say that such a thing
simply should not exist, and having now tried one, I must
say I am in complete agreement with them.

At least the company outdoes the pizza. When the conversation eventually comes around to my cycle ride and getting
lost, the Brit offers me his computer and Internet access to plan
a route on Google Maps. His assessment of my position pretty
much concurs with Antonio's, though. No matter which direction I take tomorrow, I am, to use Antonio's word, *fucked*.

"You'll have to go over Desert Road," says the Brit.
"There's nothing out there for miles; that's why it's called
that. The military use the area for training. It's usually closed
in the winter because the road is too dangerous to cross. It
should be open now it's spring, but be sure to take enough
water and food. You'll pass some volcanic mountains. It's a
very long uphill climb, but there are some incredible views."

None of this sounds very encouraging. "What about
heading west and following the coast that way?"

"No point now. You'll still have to cross mountains. And that way would be even worse. Trust me, the Desert Road's your best option. You're here, so you might as well see the best of the country."

SEPTEMBER 6, 2012

Slugging up the volcanic mountain plateau, I wonder if the Desert Road really is the best option. When he said it would be "a long uphill climb," I never imagined anything could be *this* long. I've been climbing steadily for a good eighty miles with little reprieve. The only food I've eaten, apart from bagels and cream cheese for breakfast, is some protein bars I brought with me from America. I stupidly assumed there would be at least a few service stations en route where I could find more food and water.

My muscles are shaking with fatigue. I dismount often to stretch out the cramps in my thighs, helplessly wondering how I will continue if it keeps on like this for much longer. I have no way of knowing where I am or where the nearest town might be. There is only one thing I can do: just keep pedaling.

The wind, which has been behind me most of the day, has now changed direction and is sweeping down the snow-capped mountains in a westerly direction. There are strong wind warning signs on the road for the trucks—and I soon understand why they're necessary. The gusts grow ever stronger as the sun sets, blasting into me at well over sixty miles an hour. After being blown off the road twice, I'm forced to dismount and walk.

The temperature plummets with the encroaching darkness. As long as I was pedaling, I kept reasonably warm. But now, in addition to being inadequately dressed for subzero temperatures, my clothes are drenched with sweat. The wind is so strong, it lifts Pegasus off the ground, bags and all. Staggering slowly along, trying to keep on my feet, for the first time I begin to experience real concern for my safety. I've lost all feeling in my extremities, and my body is shaking uncontrollably, leading me to worry that I may be in the early stages of hypothermia.

When Antonio calls, the only sound is the wind in my ears.

"I can't hear anything!" I shout into the phone. "If you can hear me, I don't know where I am. But the next town can't be far. I'll call you when I get there." *If* I get there. There's no point telling him I'm in serious trouble. What could he possibly do? Without the tracker, he can't even pinpoint my location on the map; he'll just stay up all night in a nervous panic if I reveal how desperate I am.

In the murky darkness ahead, I spot a camper van parked on the opposite side of the highway. The silhouette of a woman is framed in the window. The neon light reflects off her silver hair like a halo, and she appears, in that fortuitous moment, like a saving angel. I cross the road and knock on the window. She looks up from the dishes she is washing, smiles, and waves, as though a cyclist banging on her window is a perfectly normal, everyday event.

"*Help!*" I shout through the wind.

She signals for me to come around to the other side of the camper van, and as she unlocks and opens the door, a powerful gust slams it hard against the side panel.

"Oh my. Oh dear! What a wind!" she hollers, coming down the steps.

"P-please, I need some help," I say, the teeth tap-dancing in my mouth. "I think . . . I'm g-g-getting hypothermic."

"Oh, you poor thing! What on earth are you doing out here in this weather in the dark? Oh—oh my!" Another powerful gust blasts against us. She reels about and grabs hold of the side of the camper van.

"I was cycling over the Desert Road, b-but the wind got too strong to keep pedaling. I d-d-don't know how far it is to the nearest town."

"Are you alone?"

I nod.

"You must be crazy."

Her husband—gray-haired and ruddy-complexioned—peers out. "Hullo! Everything all right?"

"N-no, n-n-not really." My teeth are chattering uncontrollably now.

"The poor thing got stuck out here in the dark," his wife explains. "Why don't you come inside for a cuppa and get warm."

"Yes, everybody inside," her husband agrees. "This is no weather to be out in."

"What about my b-b-bike?"

"Uh, well, we can put it in the back."

He opens the rear storage compartment and helps me lift Pegasus inside. Then we all pile into the camper van.

"I'm Trevor, and this is my wife Pat," he says. They had pulled off the road to eat dinner and were just clearing up when I chanced upon them.

"I'm Juliana."

"Oh, look at you, you poor dear! You're shaking. What can we get you? A nice hot cuppa?" Pat offers.

"Forget the tea. A bit o' bourbon will do her better," Trevor suggests, and I could not agree more. He reaches into the cabinet for the bottle and pours me a glass. "There you go. Get that into you."

No further encouragement is necessary. I obediently knock back the fiery liquor. Meanwhile Pat puts a kettle on the stove, and while she prepares the tea, Trevor pours me a second shot of bourbon. I can feel warmth suffusing my body, extremities tingling as the blood rushes into them. By the time I'm drinking the tea, I'm already pretty well heated up.

"Now then," Trevor, who has been watching me from across the little foldout table, says, "tell us, what are you doing all alone out here on a bicycle?"

"I'm cycling across the North Island."

"You're *what*?"

"Cycling from Auckland to Wellington."

"All alone?"

"Yup."

"What for?"

It's not the first time I've been asked this question. "Uh,

well . . . because I'm cycling around the world, and New Zealand is en route."

Trevor just stares at me blankly. Then he starts laughing. "You . . . are . . . cycling . . . around . . . the *world*?"

"Yes."

Pat sits down next to her husband, shaking her head. "You're plum mad."

"You're probably right."

"Why?" Trevor asks again.

"Why not?" I smile.

"No, seriously."

"Well, I'm hoping to set the first women's record for cir-cumnavigating the world by bicycle." I explain all the details, the route, the rules, and everything else they want to know. While we chat, Pat prepares some sausages and butters bread for my dinner. She reminds me of my German *oma*—my grandmother on Mum's side. Gentle, caring, and attentive.

My *oma* and *opa* came to Greece to visit when I was a baby and Mariana was a one-year-old toddler. We were living in a big commune on the beach in Rafina just outside of Athens. Dad had created a radio program—*Music with Meaning*—that was broadcast on more than two thousand stations around the world, and anybody in the group who could play an instrument or sing was sent to Rafina to create music for the show. Mum was a violinist on the show, and when Dad fell ill, she was assigned to care for him. They fell in love, and I was the result, followed by my brother, Victor.

Mum suffered from a rare form of arthritis that wors-
ened with every pregnancy, and after Lily was conceived her
condition deteriorated to the point where she could barely
walk. This was reason enough for the cult leaders to separate her from my father. Dad was the star of the show, and
they did not want his attention and loyalty distracted by a
private love affair and a growing family. Mum was sent back
to Germany with my brother and two sisters for treatment.
She was forced to leave me behind at four years old, and I
didn't hear from her again until I was allowed to visit her
briefly for the first time at fourteen.

I did not see my grandparents again until I was seventeen,
when I decided to visit them on my own for a week. They had
always wondered what became of me and were thrilled when
I contacted them. After Mum returned to Germany with my
siblings, I had simply vanished from their lives, as though I'd
never existed. Meeting my grandparents was an emotional
experience for me. I didn't recognize their faces, but they had
saved stacks of photographs of me and the rest of the family
from my early childhood. I had been forced to destroy all my
photographs, so this was the first time I saw pictures of my
mother, father, brother, and sisters all together.

One evening Oma and Opa went out, leaving me alone in
their living room. The soundtrack to the film *Somewhere in
Time* was playing on the old record player. As I sat cross-
legged on the wooden floor, looking through photo albums
of distant and close family members, a profound sadness
swept over me—the kind I had often felt on waking from a
recurring childhood dream. In the dream I would see my

mother in the distance, holding my brother and sister by the hand. I'd call out to them—louder and louder—but they couldn't hear me. They just kept walking away from me as I desperately tried to catch up. No matter how fast I ran, they always moved farther into the distance. I would wake up sobbing hysterically, my mattress soaked in sweat.

That evening in Germany, as I looked at a picture of my smiling two-year-old self, a feeling of deep bereavement hit me like a sucker punch to the gut. That happy little girl did not know the trials she was about to face, the sense of abandonment, and the trauma of growing up alone in a frightening world, never knowing from where the next blow would come, with no one to protect her, nobody to run to for help, nobody to offer her solace from the suffering. A giant sob shook my body and emerged in a loud, anguished cry. I hadn't allowed myself to cry for years, but the tears came flooding out. Once I started, I couldn't stop. I wept for hours, mourning the family, the childhood, and the innocence that a little girl had irretrievably lost.

I stayed with my grandparents for a week and for the first time understood what it meant to have family who truly cared for me. It gave me a glimpse into everything I had missed over the previous fourteen years. I reconnected with my mother again shortly afterward and celebrated my eighteenth birthday with her and my brother and sisters.

"My goodness, you were hungry," Pat says as I polish off the sausages and buttered bread.

The next obvious question is *What now?*

"How far is the nearest town?" I ask Trevor.

"Well, about ten miles in that direction." He points with a thumb over his shoulder, indicating the road leading down the mountain.

"Do you think the wind will die down a bit?"

"Not likely. It will probably be like this till morning."

"Great," I sigh. "Do you think you might be able to drop me there? I'll just have to ride back up here tomorrow and start again."

Trevor does not appear keen to head back the way they have just come. They were planning to drive another 125 miles in the opposite direction, to stay the night with friends. We toss around a few ideas, then he slaps both hands decisively down on the table. "Look, it makes no sense for you to go down there and come back again. We'll stay parked here, and you can sleep the night if you don't mind the bunk up there." Once again he points a thumb over his shoulder, this time indicating a little cubicle above the driver's seat. It might just as well be a king-size bed in a five-star hotel, so shattered am I from the day's exertions.

"That looks wonderful. I could sleep just about anywhere. Are you sure, though? I really don't want to inconvenience you."

"Not a problem. If you're fine with that, we'll call our friends and let them know we won't arrive till tomorrow."

"I really appreciate it. *Thank you!*"

"You'll probably want to eat some breakfast before you leave in the morning," Pat says. "What time will you wake up?"

"I usually get up at dawn, so around six. Don't worry about breakfast, though. I can get something in town when I arrive there."

"It's no trouble. We'll get up around then ourselves, so you might as well eat with us."

SEPTEMBER 7, 2012

True to her word, Pat is up at dawn, preparing coffee and toast with butter and honey. I eat quickly, pack up Pegasus, and say goodbye to my rescuers. The wind, though still strong, has dropped off considerably. More to the point, it's now behind me. After a good nine-hour sleep, I feel completely recovered and ready for today's challenges.

Yesterday morning I made a short phone video and posted it to my Facebook page to let people know that I've run out of money so will have to fly home shortly. I had hoped that leaving without a sponsor would prove my serious intention to cycle the world, and that some company or other would invest in me once I was under way. I now realize that this was overly optimistic.

No sooner had the video uploaded than I started to receive messages from online supporters who'd been following my adventures, telling me not to worry about the money, to keep going. Antonio calls to tell me donations have been flooding in, and we now have enough to continue on to Australia. Buoyed by this unexpected good news, I book an early morning flight to Brisbane for September 9.

Despite the misadventures and series of unfortunate events that have made up the bulk of my New Zealand experience thus far, I've been well compensated by cycling through countryside that can be described only as otherworldly. It is clear why Kiwi director Peter Jackson chose his home country as the setting for Middle Earth in his epic *Lord of the Rings* trilogy. I keep expecting to bump into a pipe-smoking hobbit emerging from one of the many strangely shaped hills carpeted in vivid greens and yellows. Angry crosswinds whip the clouds into dramatic formations; rivers flow into waterfalls that charge over craggy bluffs. The whole place has an eccentric, haunting beauty. I feel as if I've stepped through a portal into another world.

SEPTEMBER 8, 2012

I turn on the television and catch today's local weather report. Powerful winds of up to 100 miles per hour and heavy rain are predicted for one p.m. Wellington isn't called "The Windy City" for nothing. Although less than promising, the good news is that the gale-force winds will be mostly behind me. I just have to reach the airport before one p.m.

This seems simple enough in theory. But the reality is hardly ever simple. In order to avoid pedaling along the highway—which would be direct and straightforward but illegal—my satnav takes me down numerous side roads that don't exist. I get lost a couple of times and have to retrace my steps—now *into* the wind, of course, at which point the wind and I exchange a few strong words. Nevertheless by one p.m. I am just six miles from the airport and feeling relaxed when, right on cue, the clouds explode in a downpour that would shame the fiercest Asian monsoon. The powerful torrent hits me like a fusillade of bullets.

"Oh, come *on!*" I shout into the maelstrom. There is nothing to do except embrace the deluge and keep pedaling. If you can't beat it, join it. I arrive at the airport with my body, bags, and bike completely drenched, attracting disapproving stares as I drip my way through the departures hall and into a cafeteria. I need something hot, and quickly.

Sipping a cappuccino, I check my phone messages. Mark Bennett and his wife live in Wellington, and they've been following me on Facebook. They had sent a message that suggested we meet at the airport as they knew a place nearby where I should be able to find a box for Pegasus. They're flying in today from a vacation on the South Island. I get another message from Mark, saying that their plane has been delayed, but they should be with me in an hour. My flight out to Brisbane is early tomorrow morning, which gives me a leisurely half day to disassemble and box up Pegasus and get the rest of my gear in order.

I settle down at a table in another café and grab something to eat while I wait. Just as I am finishing, Mark and his wife emerge out of arrivals, and we walk to the local bike shop not far away to pick up the box. As a keen cyclist himself, Mark has had plenty of experience pedaling through New Zealand's challenging elements.

"After hearing about your journey and your story, our

two sons have decided to donate all their piggybank savings to the Safe Passage Foundation," he tells me.

"*Wow!* How old are your sons?"

"Seven and ten."

"Please tell them thank you. I can't tell you how much that means to me."

"When does your flight leave?" he asks.

"Very early in the morning. I need to find somewhere cheap right next to the airport, if possible. I'll have to be up at around three."

I discover too late that all the hotels and hostels near the airport are booked out because New Zealand is playing an important football match tomorrow. "I guess my only option is to spend the night in the airport itself," I say after trying all of them.

"That's not even an option," Mark says. "The airport closes for a few hours every night. It reopens at four a.m."

Once again I am saved by Kiwi kindness. The Bennetts invite me to stay the night in their guest room, and Mark even arranges for his father to drive me to the airport early the next morning. I have my first warm bath in over a week, wash and dry all my clothes, and clean and pack Pegasus in readiness for the 3,250-mile journey across Australia. I feel fresh stirrings of anticipation. This adventure thing is becoming addictive.

KAMIKAZE MAGPIES

SEPTEMBER 9, 2012

Jesse meets me at Brisbane's arrivals hall and waits patiently while I reassemble Pegasus. He hasn't changed since I last saw him ten years ago in the Gambia: tall and well built, with black hair and Asian features. I was visiting Mariana and Lily in Senegal, and we had taken a bush taxi over the border into the Gambia, where Victor was living with Jesse, his wife Maria, and their baby son. They were all struggling to survive as missionaries. With no field support in that impoverished country, they had difficulty raising money for even the most basic necessities, so they ate a lot of boiled eggs and peanuts—the cheapest food available. Finally, when their son almost died from a serious illness and Maria got pregnant again, they decided enough was enough and returned to their home country, Australia.

I follow Jesse's car out of the airport. The route to Brisbane is confusing in itself, and finding a road that is cyclable even more so.

"One of my cycling friends, Mick, wants to pedal part of the way with you," Jesse informs me when we stop at a shopping center.

I recognize Mick when he pulls up on his shiny black road bike. His face is older, but the sandy blond hair, blue eyes, and distinctive nose are all unmistakable. "I know you!" I shout.

"You do?"

"Don't you remember me from Japan?"

Mick had attended the school in Tateyama, Japan, where I was sent at eight years of age. The cult leaders had separated him from his parents, just as they had separated me from mine, so he often ended up in the same training centers—disguised as "international schools"—that were created specifically to condition and indoctrinate children born into the group. I was not yet six when I was sent to the largest one, in the Philippines, and herded into a group of thirty-five other children of the same age. It was the first of many such centers to sprout up around the world. They all used food and sleep deprivation, beatings, "exorcisms," enforced silence, and public humiliation to mold an army of "little soldiers for Christ." I learned to shout "Revolution for Jesus!" at the top of my voice, never to question any instruction or doctrine, and never to form any attachment to my fellow inmates, family, or even possessions. Most chillingly, I was taught to embrace the concept of death through martyrdom.

The Children of God were an apocalyptic cult, and they lived in anticipation of the imminent end of the world. Any day now, we were told, the Great Tribulation would begin, and the Anti-Christ and his forces would take over the world for seven years. During this time we would have to go into hiding. If we were captured, we would probably be tortured and eventually killed. The Christian martyrs of times past were our childhood heroes. Many bedtime stories featured such macabre scenarios as Daniel's ordeal in the den of lions, being sent naked onto a frozen lake, being shot or burned alive—all to prepare our young hearts and minds for death before we could even start to think about life. At the time the notion of living into my thirties seemed just as incredible as living forever. We were born old, waiting to die, reconciled to the idea that life was just a commercial break of sacrifice and suffering, here for a moment, then gone like a bad idea, a blink in the eternal paradise of the afterlife.

I cried on my thirtieth birthday. When Antonio asked me what was the matter, I told him, "I wasn't supposed to get old!"

He thought I was hysterical. "You're only thirty!" he said, laughing.

The eight-year-old me would never have dreamed she would eventually grow up and ride a bicycle around the world.

"I'll leave you guys to catch up," Jesse says as he drives off, leaving Mick and me to start our ride together. "See you at my house later?"

Jesse's place is forty-five miles down the coast. After

thirty-five miles, I have my first breakdown. The shifter must have been damaged during the flight because the derailleur has jammed deep into the spokes. "Shit." I carry Pegasus to a café across the road while Mick calls Jesse.

"Okay, the good news is that he's coming right over, and there's a bike shop not far from here," Mick says as he disconnects.

I treat myself to a consolatory piece of cake while we wait for Jesse to turn up, which he does just ten minutes later. We leave Pegasus at the bike shop, and Jesse drives us to his place, where Maria is waiting with cold beers. She shows me around their spacious, tastefully decorated home. The kitchen leads out to a veranda with a large garden beyond. What a difference from when last I met them in Africa! Jesse is now in IT, and Maria is studying for a degree while also working part time at their boys' school.

The four of us sit in the garden with our beers, and Jesse fires up the barbecue. I enjoy the easy feeling of hanging out with family. We all shared the same unusual upbringing, one that most people would consider bizarre at best; but when we're with each other, we don't have to explain anything. We know who we are and where we came from. Our home was not a house, a neighborhood, a city, or a country; it was not even a person. Home, for us, was a group, a collective identity that spoke the same language, used the same lingo, sang the same songs, and followed the same belief system. As long as you spoke, sang, and thought the same way, you belonged to it.

Now, however, we come from nowhere. We blend in

everywhere, yet never really belong anywhere. With a shared history as intangible as a waking dream, we find each other in Internet chatrooms, where we swap stories and stupid slogans like children trading shiny stickers, desperate to confirm that our memories are real, that our strange childhoods did actually happen.

No matter where I go around the world, I can always find the same unspoken understanding. It's like belonging to a secret society. We take care of one another for no other reason than our shared cultural identity, even though it's one that most of us would prefer to forget.

SEPTEMBER 10–11, 2012

Jesse cycles the first miles down the Gold Coast with me. Most of the roads have spacious cycle paths, something I did not encounter often in Europe or the United States. "Drivers don't have much patience for cyclists here, so be careful," Jesse says as he waves goodbye and peels off the highway to go to work, leaving me alone on the road to Sydney.

It's dead flat as I head south along the east coast, which makes for fast cycling, especially when coupled with a pleasant tailwind. Pegasus has a new rear derailleur, my legs are feeling strong, and I'm in a great mood. The sun is shining high overhead when I notice the shadow of a bird hovering. Then it swoops down, flapping next to me, squawking conversationally.

"Well, good morning to you too, Mr. Birdie. You're

awfully friendly. What the—!" With a warning screech, my feathered friend plunges headlong into my helmet. I remember hearing stories of infamous magpie attacks in Australia and rather belatedly put two and two together. So this is a magpie, and I am not, after all, a bird whisperer. I wave one hand over my head and pedal hard as the bird continues to circle, looking for an opportunity to swoop again. It gives up after a few miles, but another soon takes its place. It is early spring, peak nesting time, and magpies across the country are all on high intruder alert.

There is plenty of advice and information on the subject of magpie attacks. Apparently the birds are able to recognize faces, and they don't attack familiar local residents. Passing around-the-world cyclists are obviously fair game, though. They also seem to hate helmets: in one study, they targeted helmeted cyclists while leaving bareheaded ones alone. I am not about to take mine off to confirm that theory, particularly as it's the only thing standing between their beaks and my skull.

I reach the small coastal town of Evans Head at sunset. Strolling down the quiet, empty roads to find something to eat, I end up at a pub where I am promptly invited to join the self-proclaimed "Publican," "Lunatic" and "Gigolo." This diverting trio try to keep me entertained throughout dinner: the Publican with free refills; the Gigolo with smooth come-ons; and the Lunatic with off-color jokes. At the end of the evening, the Publican of this fine establishment presents me with a Bundaberg rum key ring as a parting gift.

"I just want to give you something so you won't forget

us," he explains, then slides a shot of the famous local rum liquor across the counter to me.

I suddenly realize why I've been pedaling through fields of sugarcane all day. I tear myself away from the trio's endearing company with great difficulty. In their minds, having to get up at dawn to cycle 125 miles is a poor excuse to end the night so early.

SEPTEMBER 12, 2012

It is with even greater difficulty that I rouse myself at six a.m. and hit the road with some Metallica blaring to get my legs pumping. The pounding rock music fills my ears, so I don't hear the furious barking of a guard dog as it tears across the road toward me from a nearby farm. I do, however, feel its wet jaws snap at my ankle as it tries to lock on.

"Wooooaaahhhh!" I shout, as much in surprise as in the vague hope that a high-pitched holler might startle the dog long enough for me to dash out of chomping range. My adrenaline soars in a seismic spike as I pedal hard, fangs still snapping close at my heels.

No sooner have I outridden the dog and my heart rate has slowed than I hear the telltale preplunge shriek of yet another magpie. *Great.* I pick up the pace once more, waving one frenetic arm overhead. Unsure whether the bird is still around, I continue to flap my hand for the next few miles, just in case.

By midday I've suffered five magpie attacks, with the

more desperate of them dive-bombing, kamikaze style, straight into my helmet. I am beginning to develop a complex. Every shadow and birdcall sees me hunched over and waving like a lunatic. Faces in passing cars stare out at me curiously. Some wave back. But if I look like a crazy person, I hardly care. A special freedom comes with not worrying about what people think. Imagine what would happen if one day everybody stopped caring, though. Something out of a Dickensian madhouse comes to mind.

SEPTEMBER 15, 2012

I reached the periphery of Sydney yesterday and decided to circumnavigate the city by taking Putty Road, the scenic route through Yengo National Park, which borders the Blue Mountains. Maneuvering through big cities is a great time-consumer. I always try to avoid it because I tend to get lost. My sense of direction is good out on the open road, where I can follow the sun and know whether I am heading the right way. A loose route plan with the names of major roads and towns along the way is all I really need. But put me in a city, and I am as confused as a toddler in a giant shopping center. Up, down, left, and right—it all looks the same. Few things are more stressful than trying to find your way through a metropolitan maze on a bicycle.

Much like New Zealand's Desert Road, there is nothing on Putty Road for over eighty miles. Remembering how I fared last week, Antonio was less than thrilled with my route choice, especially when I mentioned feeling feverish and weak when we spoke at the start of the day. "What if something happens to you? What if you get *really* sick? You'll be in the middle of nowhere, with nobody to help you."

"The other choice is to follow the coast, which would mean passing through the center of Sydney. Putty Road is the better option."

"Please, Ju, don't go that way. It's not a good idea."

So of course, I headed that way.

And of course, there is no phone connection out here. By nightfall, I find myself once again in freezing temperatures, without water, in pitch blackness with my headlight battery nearly dead, and no idea of how far I am from civilization. The one thing of which I am absolutely certain is that Antonio is developing ulcers, and his first words when he finally manages to reach me on the phone will be "I *told* you!"

Unlike in New Zealand, though, I am not particularly worried. Antonio knows which road I'm on, and he knows the number for my two childhood friends who live nearby—Ruth and Marty—who have invited me to stay the night. I'm confident that he will rouse a search party when he fails to hear from me, which is exactly what he does. Only it's not Ruth and Marty who find me first. Up ahead the headlights of an approaching car are illuminating the road. It slows down and pulls over, and the silhouette of a waving woman gets out. As I ride closer, I can make out a long-haired brunette who looks remarkably like Cher sans the plastic surgery.

"Juliana!" she says. "I'm Karen—Donna's friend." After

putting me up in Seattle, Donna alerted some of her friends along the rest of my route. Karen lives in the Blue Mountains, and she's driven down to find me on the road.

"You've come at a good time," I tell her. "I have no idea how much farther it is to the nearest town, but I'm pretty cold and thirsty, and my light is about to die. I expect my friends are coming to find me, but I can't contact them. There's no cell signal."

"Well, there's a service station a few miles farther down the road. I saw a little cafeteria next to it. We could go and have a drink and use their phone. I'll show you where it is."

"That'd be perfect."

Near the station, I get one signal bar on my phone, so I can contact Ruth and tell her where I am. Karen treats me to some food while we wait and I hear her life story. She uses a lot of hippy talk, with words like "sister" and "man" cropping up frequently.

"I've brought some stuff I want to give you. You ever hear of maca root? It's an incredible energy and mood booster." She tells me she pulled out of menopausal depression after she started taking the magical root and she thinks it will do wonders for me on the road. She even has printouts of articles explaining the benefits of the wonder food. "Don't take my word for it," she says. "Try it for yourself. Apparently athletes who use it can go twenty percent longer than their counterparts." Then she pulls out a brown bag of powdered maca root. I've never heard of the stuff before this evening, but if it does even half of what she claims, I'm willing to give it a go.

A face suddenly peers in at us through the window. Ruth has found me! Her expression is one of relief, and she signals a thumbs-up to Marty in the car. She comes straight in and gives me the kind of long, tight hug you would give a missing child at the lost and found. Her tension is palpable.

"I'm guessing Antonio called you?"

"Yeeeees." She starts to laugh.

"In a panic?"

"*Yes!* He insisted we drop everything immediately and come to look for you."

"Thought he might. Poor Antonio. I'm always doing this to him."

"Well, we're just glad you're all right. After speaking with him, we thought you'd be in some kind of desperate trouble."

"What can I say? He's a Neapolitan. Keeping calm is not exactly his strong point."

Karen says goodbye after a round of beers, and we put Pegasus into the back of Ruth and Marty's car. Marty drives, and Ruth pulls out a bottle of whiskey. She must have read the memo.

"Before we talk, get this down you," she says, pouring me a glass.

"Only if you're joining me."

"Absolutely."

We drink all the way down the mountain road. There's so much to say, but it can all wait, because in this moment we are young again and some things never change. It's been almost twenty years since we were kids together in Thailand. At nine years old, Ruth and I were sent to the same training center in Samut Prakan, on the periphery of Bangkok, together with some two hundred other kids. Marty was there, too—a couple of years younger, in the group under ours. Whereas most of the children got to see their parents once a week, we never saw ours. Like my father, Ruth's parents worked for the leaders. Like me, she was labeled a rebel.

Warm and bathed, we sit in her kitchen over dinner and a bottle of wine.

"I remember when you were sent to live with your father in Japan at thirteen years old and came back from the school there a year later," Ruth recalls. The 21st Century International School, in Tateyama, was considered one of the more "progressive" training centers at the time. Many of the cult's videos and teaching materials were created there, and the pupils were allowed to wear fashionable clothes and makeup. As a result, our Southeast Asian counterparts considered us tainted or "worldly." "I was so happy to see you again, but then the teachers told us that we weren't allowed to speak to you, because you were 'out of the spirit.'"

I was considered a potential troublemaker who might put rebellious or "open-minded" ideas into the heads of my peers. As a preventive measure, I was punished and isolated without ever committing a "crime." This included hard labor—carrying rocks, digging ditches, sweeping, mopping, waxing, and buffing the entire one-third-of-a-mile building. Then there was the enforced silence, suspension from playing sports, and daily written reports on all my thoughts, words, and actions.

But that is a story for another day. Another lifetime, maybe. Chatting with Ruth about it now feels a lot like sharing prison stories with another ex-inmate. After dinner she whips up an old childhood treat that we called "rice cereal"— a thick milk powder paste mixed into a bowl of rice. The more milk powder, the better. We ate the stuff as a snack twice a day, every day, as kids. It's strange sitting together again now as adults, eating rice cereal and reliving memories that seem fantastic at best.

Ruth tells me about her struggle to figure out life and get started in the "outside" world. She and Marty married while still in the group and decided to leave the same year I did. They arrived in Australia with their three kids in the middle of winter with just three hundred dollars and clothes they thought were warm. Marty's first job was as a kitchen hand, washing dishes. He would walk the two miles to work and back as they had no money for the bus fare, let alone a car.

"I think rock bottom came the night Marty twisted his ankle going to work," remembers Ruth. "It got progressively worse throughout the night, and by the time he finished work he couldn't walk. He had no money for a taxi, and since we didn't have a phone, he couldn't even call me. He tried hopping, but the vibrations made the pain worse, so he ended up crawling all the way home on his hands and knees. We are doing well now. We have money to buy nice things. But I think that knowing what it means to struggle, to pull yourself up from nothing, makes these moments of success so much sweeter."

Once again I think, *There is no satisfaction in achievement without struggle.*

SEPTEMBER 16, 2012

Today I have returned to Putty Road—to the exact spot where I encountered Cher's doppelgänger last night. Marty is a motorbike buff, and he explains that this is a popular road with bikers. He has ridden it a few times at night himself. Every five to ten minutes motorbikes race around the bends, often in large groups. I assume they have come up here for the scenic ride and the empty road. I can see the attraction of biking, the rush you get from speeding down an open road. Even from a touring aspect, it beats being in a car, watching it all pass by from behind the glass, insulated from the sounds, the smells, and the elements, like seeing the world on a TV screen. On a motorbike, there is no barrier between you and the environment: you can feel the wind, you can smell the smells. But you are still in fast forward. Speeding by, you cannot possibly notice all the small things.

On a bicycle, you are *inside* the movie, an essential part of it. Completely reliant upon your environment, you observe and absorb every sensation around you. You feel every change in terrain, the texture of the road, the direction of the wind, every ascent and descent, the constantly shifting weather. You smell every plant and flower, every rotting roadkill carcass. You hear every birdcall, every insect and animal. You take in the country, and the country takes you in.

If you really want to experience the world, get on a bicycle.

Australia has to be the most costly country I have passed through to date. Just a coffee is almost five dollars. So consuming the recommended calories of two grown men each day is burning a giant hole in my wallet. The cheapest fuel I've found is the service station steak pie, which supplies an instant hit of energy and protein. Occasionally supplemented by an "everything thrown in" Oz burger, these pies have been powering me across the continent.

I am fortunate to have many friends in Australia. They have put me up along the way, which has helped to keep the costs down. Another economical sleeping option is the Australian pub, which offers basic food, board . . . and bedbugs. Every little town has at least one of these "hotels"—usually a historic building dating back to the 1800s, with high ceilings, long halls, and creaky wooden floors. Many boast a resident ghost with an endearing nickname like Nellie or Ned. I've taken to milking the pub staff for stories about their apparitions.

Tonight, in Tarcutta, I have been billeted next to the pub's infamous "ghost room," and the proprietor imparts the delightful tale of the in-house phantom: a young man, down on his luck, hanged himself in Room 31 some fifty years ago. Since then the room has been the subject of some inexplicable goings-on.

"For instance, one day, after I'd cleaned and made up the rooms, including number thirty-one," she recounts, "I closed and locked them all for the night. The place was empty at the time, as we were doing our annual spring clean, so I was surprised when the next morning I found the door to number thirty-one cracked open. The bed was a mess, like someone had slept in it."

This, she informs me, was not the first time the room had appeared haunted by a nocturnal visitor. "A few times we've had guests complain about the racket in number thirty-one, like someone was moving furniture around. Of course we never put anyone in that room, so it couldn't have been occupied."

I'm rather disappointed not to encounter any paranormal activity myself. Thirteen hours on the road means I sleep soundly—unlike the dead, who apparently do not.

SEPTEMBER 19, 2012

A fellow cyclist, Shaun, is waiting on the road outside Melbourne to accompany me into the city and guide me through the sprawling metropolis. A seasoned bike tourer, he has cycled all around Europe and the Middle East. We met in a Facebook chat group of long-distance cyclists a few months ago and have kept in touch ever since. I spot him sitting on a patch of turf by the side of the M31 highway.

"You want a cereal bar? Water?" he offers intuitively as I pull up.

I gratefully stuff down two of his bars, and then tell him, "I'll probably need to stop for something more substantial soon."

It's already three p.m., and I've pedaled 100 miles or so without stopping for food because I want to make the most of the strong tailwind and cover the fifteen miles all the way to Melbourne. Fatigue is starting to creep up on me now, though. We spot a Subway along the highway and pull over for a late lunch. It's here that I discover their luscious brownie, and my chocolate love affair officially begins. One is simply not enough. From now on all brownies will be purchased and eaten in pairs.

The sun is just disappearing below the horizon when our wheels touch the city periphery. Shaun knows all the scenic cycle routes to avoid the worst of the traffic. It's a nice change to be pedaling next to another person. Time flies by faster— or at least the hours in the saddle are less tedious—with company. Another friend, Vincent, has offered to host me for the night, and he is waiting by Shaun's house when we arrive.

In addition to being an excellent navigator, Shaun is a bit of mechanic. He takes Pegasus off my hands to give him a tweak-over. "I'll have him ready for you bright and early tomorrow," he promises.

We arrange a time to meet in the morning, and Vincent whisks me off for a steak dinner—the surefire way to a hungry cyclist's heart. He has recently moved to Australia with his Taiwanese girlfriend, and they put me up in their guest room for the night. While my dirty clothes spin in the washing machine, a bottle of Johnnie Walker is whipped out for a nightcap. I couldn't ask for a better host.

SEPTEMBER 20, 2012

I return to Shaun's house to find Pegasus cleaned, greased, and tweaked. He looks shiny new, and I feel as spoiled as my bike, especially after scarfing down a second breakfast of Weetabix in Shaun's kitchen.

It starts to rain as we pedal out of the city, which is all the reason we need to stop for coffee and another couple of brownies. Melbourne reminds me of London, especially along the waterfront, and even more so under the gray clouds and steady drizzle. As the rain doesn't show much sign of letting up, we decide to hit the road anyway. The sun comes out as we leave the city perimeter, heading southwest toward Geelong. But with the sun comes a strong headwind. I'm slightly jealous when Shaun says goodbye and heads back in the opposite direction.

"You're gonna fly home," I say.

"Sorry I have to leave you to battle that headwind alone," he tells me. "I'm afraid you'll be getting a lot of strong winds in the direction you're going. Stay strong. Remember, brownies and ginger ale make everything better!"

Today marks two months on the road, 6,980 miles and six (and a half) countries. Pegasus has had thirteen punctures, three broken spoke nipples, two broken derailleurs, one broken light, two new sets of tires, and one new chain. I wonder what the count will be by the end of the ride.

THE TOUGH GET GOING

The headwinds are hitting hard. Locals have been telling me that I should expect them along the coast between Melbourne and Adelaide. Another nipple has broken, and the nearest bike shop I can find is the CrankHouse in Warrnambool.

"You can't pedal across the Nullarbor with what you've got," the owner, Stewart, announces after finding another loose nipple and hearing that I plan to cross the infamous desert. "If another one breaks, you risk the spokes snapping, and there's nothing out there for twelve hundred miles. You'll be really stuck then." He admits he is surprised I have gotten as far as I have on Pegasus. It's a beautiful racing bike, but a workhorse would have been better for a long-distance, endurance journey.

The mechanics change all the carbon nipples on the rear wheel to steel, and Stewart charges me trade price for the parts and nothing at all for the labor. He's an avid adventure cyclist himself—short and stocky, with leg muscles that indicate powerful pedal strokes. He and his wife Susan enjoy helping cyclists and travelers who pass through, and he invites me to stay the night with them. We leave his crew working on Pegasus and travel the short distance to their home, where Stewart entrusts me into the care of Susan, a nurturing, matronly woman, who promptly packs me off to the shower and shoves my smelly laundry into the washing machine.

Their eldest daughter prepares an incredible dinner of goat cheese salad, roasted sweet potatoes, and lamb chops—the kind of home cooking I've missed over the past two months. Hunger overrules manners as I wolf down every last morsel and polish the serving plates clean. A shower, clean clothes, and a king-size bed with fluffy pillows is the very definition of happiness.

SEPTEMBER 23, 2012

Stewart gets up early to see me off. "If anything happens to you within the next few hundred miles, give us a ring and we'll come and rescue you," he assures me, fixing a sticker with the shop's details onto Pegasus's frame.

People keep warning me of the probable dangers I face traveling across Australia as a lone woman, but so far I've encountered only the kindness and generosity of strangers along the road. And the farther south I go, the nicer they seem to get.

Many South Australians are descendants of hard-working German migrants who came over to colonize and farm the land in the nineteenth century. I encounter one of them as I pedal into Dartmoor in search of water. The only shop in the pristine town is shut, and the next settlement is another thirty-five miles down the road. An old woman in overalls, loading some boxes into her gray van, notices me trying the shop door and finding it locked. "You lookin' for something?" she asks. Her silver hair is tied up under a blue bandanna, with a few wisps floating loose around the deep lines of her face.

"Uh, yeah. Do you know if the shop will open again?"

"Afraid not. The owner's just left for the day. We're a small town, see. He doesn't stay open all hours. What were you after?"

"Something to drink."

"Well, I got a bottle of rainwater in the van if you want that."

"Sure. Thanks."

She hands me a two-liter white plastic jerrycan, and I start to drink.

"How's that taste? Not bad, huh? Collected straight off my roof."

I pause midchug. "Your roof?"

When she said "rainwater," she really did mean rainwater.

"Uh-huh. Doesn't get any fresher than that."

"No. I guess not. It isn't . . . um . . . well . . . dirty, is it?"

"*Dirty?* Not a bit." She sounds slightly miffed. "Comes

straight from the sky, passes through a filter. I've been drinking rainwater since I was a child. Water is a precious commodity out here, you know."

"Oh, yes. I know." I've learned that on the road. It's cheaper to drink beer in Australia.

"Where're you pedaling to?"

"Perth."

She starts to laugh. "No kidding. Where'd you start?"

"Brisbane."

"*Alone?*"

"Yup."

Her ice-blue eyes examine me suspiciously from head to toe, as if she is trying to make up her mind whether I'm putting her on. From her expression, she clearly thinks I'm joking, nuts, or both.

"Where are you from?"

Not *that* question again. To save time, I opt for evasion. "I'm of German origin."

She latches onto this information, as I had guessed she would. "Our ancestors were German farmers who worked this land for generations." Then like any good German, she methodically interrogates me about every detail of my travels, right down to my route plan. "You want to get to Mount Gambier today? That's a good thirty-five miles away, and you've only got about two hours of daylight left, and strong headwinds."

"Don't worry, I'll get there."

She shakes her head with an indulgent chuckle. "Didn't anybody tell you, dear? You're going the wrong way."

I can only grunt back.

"Well, I guess you'll want to get moving if you're going to reach the next town before dark. Whatever you do, don't travel at night. People disappear in the outback."

She is not the first Aussie to express concern for my safety. Everywhere I go, I'm told all manner of horror stories about tourists disappearing or being killed by outback nutters. "Haven't you seen *Wolf Creek*?" they all ask. Based on the true story of two backpackers who were tortured and killed some years back, the film is a popular reference for scaring off the wary traveler entering the remote wilderness that is the Australian outback. I have no intention of seeing this film, now or ever. It would be like someone on a plane watching a film about 9/11.

"Good luck to you, dear," she calls, getting into her van.

I wave and pedal off in the direction of Mount Gambier while she drives away in the other. So needless to say, I'm surprised when I spot her gray van at the side of the road minutes later. She is standing next to it, waving me down. How the hell did she get there without passing me?

As I ride up, she says, "I just wanted to ask, what road are you taking to Adelaide?"

"Well, I was thinking of following the coast. I'm told it's quite scenic."

"Oh *nooo*, dear. I wouldn't go that way. It's very deserted, and you're traveling alone. I recommend you go inland, where there are more towns and more traffic on the roads."

I decide this is probably good advice from a local woman

who clearly knows her way around, so I replan my route accordingly.

The closer I get to Adelaide, the stronger the headwind becomes. Today is the toughest yet. I find myself shouting at the wind, frustration mounting as the day wears on. Eventually, perhaps inevitably, comes the moment when I hit what many marathon runners call "the wall." As hard as my legs are pedaling, the bicycle is simply not moving. Another gust of wind slams into me, accompanied by sheets of icy rain. My shoes are heavy with water, squishing between my toes as I labor against the pedals. It has taken me eight hours to cover just sixty miles.

A jeep roars by, throwing up a mist of muddy spray. I mumble a few choice words, wipe the mud from my face, and tuck my glasses into my pocket. They are useless at this point. I think about the people in that jeep, windows rolled up, heating and radio on, oblivious to the elements. I would give my last chocolate peanut butter bar to be in that car right now. I'm so cold that I can no longer think about anything else. My body is shaking; my hands and feet are completely numb. This is cyclist agony, the part nobody ever mentions. There is nothing redeeming in this kind of torment. This is the moment when I wonder *why*. Why am I cycling the world? Why am I forcing my legs to continue pumping up and down, up and down, for ten to twelve hours every day?

Pain, misery, and struggle all teach you a lot about yourself. About who you are and what you are capable of under extreme conditions. I try to take my mind off the physical environment and step outside the immediate discomfort of the present. I picture a series of perfect moments. A stunning sunset. The peak of a mountain. A glass of spiced rum. Hendri's eyes. His kiss. At times of complete agony, physical and mental, these moments of perfection stand out like beacons in a stormy sea, perhaps heightened because of the contrast.

Do I endure the struggle simply to experience more extreme pleasure from these perfect moments? Perhaps that is the point. The more adversity we suffer in life, the more we savor the brief, rare periods of complete happiness and abandon. Those moments when everything—taste, sense, sight, smell, touch—is so enhanced. I think only those who know deep suffering can truly appreciate its opposite.

In this moment I realize that there is no other place I would rather be. Because of that gnawing hunger that grows with every passing mile, the next food I eat will be the most delicious in the world. The cold and wet will make the dry and warm a pleasure that surpasses all others. The fatigue in every limb will make my sleep deep and dreamless, and I will wake refreshed, ready to tackle another day with an unknown destination, new sights, endless possibilities, and even more perfect moments.

The sun is setting, and I'm about ten miles from Cooman-dook when I hear an explosion like a small bomb going off and feel the now-familiar grating of metal rim on tarmac. I get off to inspect the damage and find a jagged hole the size of my thumb in the rear tire. What makes a tire explode? There is no visible rock or glass on the road that could have caused such a gigantic tear, so I guess it has something to do with my tires wearing thin. I am in the middle of nowhere, without a spare, but I know there are parts waiting for me in Coomandook. I just have to find a way to get there, prefer-ably before sundown. I stick out my thumb.

A pickup with two large German shepherds in the back pulls up, and the driver steps out. He is tall and lean, wear-ing a checked shirt, jeans, and a cowboy hat. My first impres-sions of people are usually pretty good. I have learned to trust my intuition and, so far, it has never steered me wrong. This guy has firm lips, steady eyes, and an honest face.

"What seems to be the problem?" he asks.

"My tire's just exploded, and I need to get to the nearest town to fix it."

"Well, first off, let's get you off the road. It's dangerous for a girl like you to be hitchhiking all alone. I'm late for my son's birthday party, but I can drop you at the roadside sta-tion just up ahead. I'm sure they can help sort you out."

"That would be great. Thanks."

He puts Pegasus in the back, with the dogs, and I get in the front. A few miles ahead we come across the promised service station with a small store. He takes the bike down and rests it against the wall. The manager is out front, offloading goods from a truck. "Hiya, Mike. I found this lady here in trouble by the side of the road. Do you think you might help her get a ride to Coomandook?

"Not a problem if she can wait ten minutes," says Mike.

"Yes, of course. Thanks."

My rescuer rushes off, but not before repeating his warning about hitchhiking alone.

Mike comes to find me ten minutes later. "Come on. I'll take you there myself. I'm not putting you in some vehicle with a stranger. We look out for each other round these parts."

He loads Pegasus into the back of his beat-up jeep, and I get in the front with his son. Coomandook is about a half-hour drive down the road, and once again I can't help but think that for all the stiff warnings I've received about the dangers of traveling through the outback alone, I've encountered nothing but exceptional kindness and generosity during my time in Australia.

About an hour after Mike drops me at the local pub, a new surprise turns up. Antonio flew into Perth a couple of days ago, and since then he has driven halfway across Australia to meet me here and shoot some photos and video of the ride. Seeing him again is wonderful and strange at the same time. It feels like it has been years, not a couple of months, since we last spoke face to face.

"You look tired," he says, giving me the once-over, "but not as gaunt as you looked in the pictures from America."

"Must be the steak pies."

Antonio has heard all the horror stories about the Australian outback and insists on accompanying me across the Nullarbor, where I will have to cross seven hundred miles of desert with nothing but a handful of sporadic outposts along the way.

"You won't see much of me, but I'll keep within a fifty-mile radius of you, just in case something happens," he says.

Much as I enjoy my solitude, it is comforting to know there will be someone nearby for this stretch of the journey.

SEPTEMBER 26, 2012

With a fresh tube and tire change this morning, Antonio drops me back at the spot where I broke down yesterday. "Call me if you need anything!" he shouts before waving and driving off. The plan is to meet in Adelaide tonight, where another ex-kid Facebook friend, Angel, has offered to put me up for the night.

SEPTEMBER 27-30, 2012

Civilization has been increasingly sparse since leaving Adelaide, but the Nullarbor really starts with a sign next to a dusty roadside garage that states LAST SHOP FOR 1000 KM. I decide it's a good idea to stock up with food and water. I plan to use the long, flat desert road along the Eyre Highway to rack up the miles, aiming for an average of 150 every day. I also just want to get it over with as quickly as possible.

Edward John Eyre, the first European to cross the Nullarbor in 1841, and whom the highway was subsequently named after, described it as "a hideous anomaly, a blot on the face of Nature, the sort of place one gets into in bad dreams." The desert plain boasts the longest straight road on earth, cutting a seemingly endless line through a monotonous landscape of calf-high shrubs. For ninety miles there is not a single tree to break up the scenery, giving the impression of moving on a treadmill. Just a short detour from the main road, however, the Great Australian Bight, the bay of the southern coastline, is dramatic and unforgettable, with steep cliffs that plunge down into the dark turquoise waters of the Southern Ocean.

There is great camaraderie among the rare travelers you meet on the Nullarbor road. I receive a honk and a wave from almost every passing motorist. One guy chases me down to ask what I am doing, then hands me fifty dollars for food. A few hours later, at one of the isolated outposts, I come across a group of retired men in matching yellow-and-green jerseys drinking beer. The Fawkin' Hawkins, as they call themselves, are a colorful group of old school friends who embark on a road trip to a different place in Australia every year. And every year they design a new jersey to mark the occasion. For all their perfunctory "gruff and rough" bad jokes and ribbing, they turn out to be pure gold. I am presented with an honorary autographed yellow-and-green jersey, together with a seventy-dollar donation.

Such occasional human encounters have been the only entertaining breaks in my otherwise monotonous journey along a dead-straight road. Even animal sightings have been rare. Live animals, that is. I have seen plenty of dead ones. Roadkill is one of the principal features of the Nullarbor road. Most animals come out at night and are hit by the giant "road trains" that speed along the highway twenty-four hours a day. Come morning, the road looks like a battlefield, littered with the fresh corpses of kangaroos, dingoes, lizards, and on one occasion even a wild camel. Only magpie roadkill makes me crack a smile and utter a snide "Tried it on a truck, did ya?" The tarmac is permanently stained with rusty streaks of old blood that is perpetually replenished with new. The smell of rotting guts baking in the sun is abominable. Long hours in the saddle are primarily occupied with dodging roadkill while holding my breath and fleeing from the giant, bee-sized horseflies that feast on the carcasses.

The horseflies have replaced the kamikaze magpies as my chief tormentors. Unlike the birds, though, they are out for fresh blood, and I'm the best living source for miles around, so they're as relentless as a herd of buffalo following a receding watercourse. Even the headwinds fail to deter them. Drafting close behind me allows them smooth access to my posterior, on which they rudely settle and nip at with their mandibles, like tiny pairs of scissors. My natural reaction is to slap them away, which makes for a wonderful scene: me, pedaling at a desperate pace, while slapping at my behind with one hand, a bit like "giddy-up horsie." Come to think of it, this may be why I have been getting so many friendly honks and waves.

I'm surprised to find a "border" between East and West Australia and wonder why the government feels it's necessary. The official who flags me down to check my saddlebag is a large mannish woman. She quickly sniffs out the bag of oranges I purchased at the start of the Nullarbor, when I rightly guessed there would be next to no affordable fruit or vegetables on the highway itself. Every piece of fruit I've seen for sale in the rest stops has been the price of a full meal in Naples, so I've been savoring just one of my prized oranges every day. The service stations that offer the only food and water along the highway appear on the horizon only every 125 miles or so, so they can—and do—charge whatever they want. I almost cry every time I have to hand over ten dollars for a bottle of water.

"You cannot bring fresh produce across the border," the official informs me sharply, whisking away my last five oranges and plonking them onto her desk through the booth window. I know my precious fruit is destined for her lunch break.

"Wait! What? Why?"

My questions seem to irritate her. "It's the law," she barks impatiently.

"I didn't even know there *was* a border, so I certainly didn't know that I couldn't take fruit through it. I'm sorry. But for future reference, can I ask why?"

"You don't need to know why. It's the law. But they can carry foreign germs and bacteria" is her clipped explanation.

"Ah, I see." She is not the kind of woman you would want to get into a fight with, and yet . . . "Can I have my oranges back, please?"

"I *told* you! You cannot carry them across this border," she answers, exasperated by my importunity.

"I won't. I'll eat them now. *Before* I cross."

She clearly did not expect this and pauses uncertainly. There is no law against what I am suggesting. Eastern Australian oranges can still be eaten in eastern Australia. With a grunt, she retrieves the bag and grudgingly hands it over. I walk a few yards away, methodically peel and eat every last orange within sight of the guard, then roll across the border with a huge smile and a swollen belly.

Cyclist 1, official 0.

OCTOBER 5, 2012

Today I am emerging from the Nullarbor and heading back into semicivilization, where there are phone signals and the price of food and water is merely unreasonably expensive, as opposed to highway robbery.

The first thing I do upon arriving in the little town of Norseman is to enter a café and order two of everything: chocolate cake, muffins with jam and cream, pie, and coffee. The woman behind the counter, uncertain I'm serious, hands me the food one plate at a time, in case I can't finish it all. I grin through the whole meal, noisily cramming down unseemly mouthfuls like a feral woman just rescued from years in the wild.

Rolling into Salmon Gums, I hit the milestone of 9,011 miles cycled: halfway around the world! It has been seventy-five days since I left home, seventy-two of which have been spent on the bike. All things considered, I am still in pretty good shape, with no serious sickness, aches, or pains. As I tell friends who ask how I'm managing the long hours in the saddle, "I've become comfortably numb." For the first time, I'm starting to believe I might just make it all the way back to Naples. There is only one way to celebrate reaching the halfway mark: two brownies and a cold beer. I am just a few days from Perth, where I will catch a flight to Singapore. Given the severely diminished state of my bank account, Asia cannot come soon enough.

OCTOBER 9, 2012

Another ex-kid, Kylie, lives in Perth and owns a couple of restaurants with her partner. They've generously arranged a night at the Margaret River Resort hotel, along with a free dinner at the Maharaja restaurant next door. After ten days in the desert, the hotel bed feels like divine intervention. Antonio and I share a room and a hearty meal with a bottle of wine in celebration of another continent crossed. He films a video of me to post online thanking all my friends and supporters who've sustained me until now.

"I'm sorry I'll have to go home so soon," Antonio tells me. I'll fly to Singapore, while he plans to stay a couple more days in Perth. "It would have been fun to follow you through Southeast Asia. I've never been."

Southeast Asia is the part of the journey I've been most looking forward to. I'm curious what my impressions will be like, returning to the countries where I spent my childhood.

OCTOBER 10, 2012

I ride into Perth airport, ask an official there to sign my logbook with the time and date, then head to Kylie's for the night, to find she has prepared an amazing spread of food and drink to welcome me and Antonio. The way people have rallied around my journey, helping me however they are able, is all that has kept me on the road. The small cash donations and the constant offers of a bed and a meal en route have enabled me to get this far. Maybe there is a bit of wanderlust in each of us, and while not everyone would quit their day job to travel around the world, people like Kylie have done everything they can to ensure that I will.

FINALLY ASIA!

It's still dark when I land at Changi Airport, Singapore. A double breakfast and two coffees later, I reassemble Pegasus and wheel him out of the fresh, air-conditioned lobby. Outside, the hot air is so humid it's difficult to breathe. Even when I'm not moving, beads of sweat soon run in rivulets down my neck and back. Cycling is preferable to standing still, because at least the warm wind brings some relief. I hit the highway as the sky begins to lighten with the first purple tints of dawn.

Cycling across the whole of Singapore takes about as long as crossing a large city—a few hours at most. In fact, the entire country really is just one extended city. The roads are pristine. I'm on the highway that heads due north to the border, to avoid passing through the city center, where I'm sure I'd get lost and meet heavy traffic. There are hardly any cars on the highway, as it's still early.

By the time the sun has fully risen over the horizon, I've already pedaled the length of the country and have crossed the border into Malaysia. Everything seems poorer here, as well as noticeably Muslim. The roads are dusty and pock-marked with potholes; the buildings are dingy and run-down. Women are covered from head to toe, and I feel uncomfortably out of place in my cycling shorts and bare arms.

I'm unsure whether cycling clothes are acceptable here but soon learn the answer from a plump girl standing behind a 7/11 service station counter. She raises a pudgy finger to point at me, eyes bulging from her round, puffy face, lips open in a wide O. Uncertain whether this display of shock and horror is directed at me, my bicycle, or both, I slink out of the shop and wheel Pegasus, bags and all, into the toilets around back.

The "squat" toilets give me reason to smile. Growing up in Southeast Asia, I never sat on a toilet with a seat until I was fourteen. To this day I still prefer to squat; propitious, since I've used more bushes than toilets on this journey. Locking the door, I dig out a pair of calf-length trousers and slip them over my shorts.

Oh, the unbearable heat! It soaks my clothes and chafes my skin, which has already broken out in a heat rash, some-thing I've not experienced since I was a young child. I remem-ber, before going to bed as a toddler, my mom would slather pink calamine lotion over the itchy red bumps that covered my body. I feel transported back to my childhood. Despite the discomfort, I'm decidedly at home in these tropical surroundings. So many memories flood into my mind, triggered by the sights and smells. Recollections of train journeys from Thailand to Malaysia. Climbing tamarind trees to pick the pods, cracking open the thin brown crusts, and working the sweet-and-sour flesh off the black seeds. Gardens of banana, mango, and jackfruit trees, giant red hibiscus flowers, pink bougainvillea. The honeysuckles I loved to pluck off one by one to suck the sweet nectar from the thin stalks.

At the first roadside coconut stand I see, I pull over for a drink. They have a sugar-cane press to extract bucketloads of sweet, light green liquid from the long stalks.

"You cycle, this very good. Very fresh," the mother of the little family business tells me, holding out a clear plastic bag full of chilled sugarcane juice.

It goes down a treat in this heat, and I feel instantly revived. I could drink two, were it not for the hassle and time I'd waste stopping at public toilets every time I needed to relieve myself. Male cyclists have a clear advantage in this respect. Every toilet break for me ticks off ten minutes as opposed to their two. So it's a fine balance between drinking enough to prevent dehydration but not too much to need the loo. In this heat, I find it preferable to err on the side of over-drinking. Another cyclist once told me that you can cycle 20 percent longer on a semifull bladder. I'm not sure whether this is true, but it makes holding it for long stretches less objectionable.

I've yet to see another cyclist on the road in Malaysia. As a foreign woman alone on a bike, I'm an anomaly and therefore a curiosity. People approach very politely with their cell phones to take selfies with me whenever I stop. I'm used to being stared at now; I just blank out other humans unless they speak to me.

Perhaps I've spent too much time in my own head, but it's becoming increasingly difficult to engage in anything more than the most basic human interaction. Alone all day, with only my thoughts for company, I'm as solitary as it's possible to be, barring living in a hermitage. I've learned a lot about myself in the long periods of silence. Without the usual comforts and safety of a familiar environment, stripped down to just the bare necessities, with no one and nothing to rely on but myself, I've felt myself changing. I'm less willing to compromise with myself or others, and less forgiving of weakness in myself. I have no time for the day-to-day trivialities that I once felt were so important, like personal grooming, petty gossip, and caring what other people think of me. I'm increasingly unable to make small talk, too. After hours of silence on the road, when I finally open my mouth to speak, I now notice how much nonsense comes out. How little of substance is ever said. Everybody talks, but nobody really says anything.

"I listen to people talk, and I can't relate," Hendri once confided to me. He had been alone in the wilds of Africa for so long that coming back to civilization was a struggle. "I've been trying to speak more and have been surprised by the amount of bullshit that comes out of my mouth at times. Makes me think I should be quiet more. So rarely does speech satisfy."

Sometimes words are inadequate to describe a certain

moment, like standing on top of that proverbial mountain and feeling completely alive: when the world beneath looks so small, when reality seems to hang by a very thin thread, when existence and the realm of possibility feel limitless. Those moments cannot be explained, only experienced. It's inside those perfect moments when I feel happiest, when I feel at peace. But they are also when I feel most alone. Strange that I should be most lonely whenever I am most happy.

OCTOBER 13, 2012

Most of Malaysia's roads are without any hard shoulders, full of dust, rubbish, motorists, animals, and pedestrians. Giant trucks pass so close that their crosswinds almost push me into the gutter. So I've decided to cycle up the E2 highway, which runs from the border with Singapore all the way to Kuala Lumpur, as it has a wide shoulder and the tarmac is perfect. But while this is the most efficient way of getting from point A to B, it's also the most illegal.

Several hours and a lot of fast miles up the road, a yellow highway patrol truck drives in front of me, blocking my path. Two policemen get out.

"What you do?" says the plumper of the two.

"I'm cycling to Kuala Lumpur."

"No, no! You no cycle this road. This is highway."

"My navigator told me to take this road."

"No, this road no good. You no can cycle highway."

"This is highway?" I say. When in doubt, play dumb.

"Yes, yes!"

"Oh. So how can I get to Kuala Lumpur?"

"You must exit. Exit ahead. You take local road."

"Okay. But I don't know where is the local road."

"You come. Follow us."

They guide me off the highway and back onto the old potholed road on which I set off this morning. Bugger.

They stop at the crossroads and get out of the truck. "This the road. You follow this road."

"Okay, thanks."

"You take photo now, please." He pulls out his phone, and both cops take turns posing next to the crazy foreign woman on a bike. "Okay, very good. You follow this road now. Okay? Bye."

I wave as they drive off. The moment their truck disappears from view, I ride to the next highway entrance and get back on again. If I could think of a safer way to reach Kuala Lumpur, I would take it. At least I'm making good time, even though I'm interrupted every few hours by a new patrol car that escorts me off the road. Every time I feign ignorance, apologize profusely, pose for selfies, then promptly return to the highway to do it all again.

I finally reach Kuala Lumpur late in the evening. Navigating through the city is a logistical nightmare. By night it looks like a party town, with flashing billboards and colorful neon lights. All the roads are similar, the one-way system is confusing, and after getting lost and turning around repeatedly, I eventually flag down a taxi driver for directions. An old friend from Kampala is now based in the city, and she has kindly offered me a bed for the night at her apartment. I show the driver the address, and he nods and signals for me to follow him. It turns out I've been really close, going around in circles for a couple of hours. I try to tip the guy for his trouble, but he just smiles and waves me off. I find the key to Kirsten's apartment hidden under a giant pot in the apartment complex entrance, just where she said it would be.

Kirsten is one of my oldest and closest friends. I think of her more as an older sister. She helped me get set up and fig-ure things out as I learned to navigate my way through the world. I was twenty-three and living in Uganda when I decided to leave the cult. Not the easiest country in which to make a start. Most of the foreigners living there worked for NGOs, banks, or multinational corporations, or else they had started their own businesses. I had no formal education or qualifications, so Kirsten helped me write up a CV and apply for my first real job, managing a large nightclub in Kampala. She was always there whenever I needed help or advice. She is another of those people I call family, even though it has been years since I have seen her.

She is not home when I arrive, but a bag of takeout food is hanging on the door for me, along with a note. Typical Kirsten, always thinks of everything. Her shower is huge, and the variety of shampoos and soaps are a luxury after days of washing with just water. Occasionally, I will use bar soap from cheap motels and hostels. My hair looks and feels like straw. I chopped it short before starting the ride, knowing that hygiene and personal maintenance would be very low on my list of priorities over the next few months.

Body scrubbed and belly full, I collapse onto the king-size bed and fall into a deep sleep.

OCTOBER 14, 2012

Kirsten came home at some point during the night, but I never heard her. It's late in the morning by the time I awake, and I don't head off before midday. There's so much catching up to do, it's hard to pull myself away and get back on the road.

It's early afternoon by the time I reach the outskirts of Kuala Lumpur, at which point the clouds explode in a torrential downpour. I keep on pedaling until Zeus-worthy lightning bolts start tearing through the sky, striking the ground just yards away. It would be rather silly to be hit by lightning. A unique way to go, granted, but I wouldn't want people shaking their heads over my ashes, muttering, "Only an idiot cycles through a lightning storm." So I join a group of motorcyclists under an overpass to wait it out.

When the worst rolls over, I get back on the road, hoping to cross the Thai border and make it to Hat Yai before dark. Dallying is not an option. If I were to stop every time it rained, I would hardly move. The monsoon season is coming to an end, but there are still afternoon showers almost every day. To keep the water out of my gear, I tie a plastic bag around the saddlebag, which mostly seems to work.

Between the rain and the endless sweating, there is never a moment when my clothes aren't totally drenched. I don't mind the wet, though, because at least it keeps my body from overheating.

I spent almost four formative years of my childhood in Thailand—from nine to twelve years old—and again, briefly, when I was fourteen. A small part of me still thinks of the country as home. I called so many places "home" when growing up that each one holds a claim on some part of my past and some facet of my identity. Some days I feel like an alien who belongs nowhere; but at other times, like today, I feel that I belong *everywhere*. I suppose I am a child of the world in the truest sense of the phrase. Today feels like coming home; I am looking forward to so many things. The food, the people, the beautiful beaches, the culture . . . but if I'm completely honest, I would have to say mostly the food.

I cross the Thai border around midafternoon and have just reached a little town near Hat Yai when the dark skies explode once again. The streets flood with so much water that they soon empty completely of people and traffic. It becomes dangerous to pedal, so I decide to join the locals and call it a day.

THE CONSEQUENCES
OF SOLITUDE

The weather forecast predicted sunny skies today, so I set off early from Sadao to make good time and clock up some extra miles. About sixty miles north of Hat Yai, my front tire goes flat. Thankfully I still have a spare tube, so I pull off the highway to change it. I used my other spare back in Malaysia after a suffering a bad puncture, courtesy of a giant nail on the highway. I've also broken another two spoke nipples, and they need changing, so finding a bike shop is becoming a top priority. It will also be nothing short of miraculous. So far I've encountered next to no cyclists in Malaysia and Thailand, which means bike shops are few and far between. Fortunately I still have plenty of tube patches and glue, so I am optimistic I will reach Bangkok before they run out.

My grip has steadily weakened from holding on to the

handlebars for hours on end, day after day, and I struggle to change the tube. Popping the tire back onto the rim becomes a ponderous ordeal. My thumbs have no strength, so I use the cumbersome lever tool to force it back on. It takes half an hour, but at last the rubber pops into place. A quick pump, and I'll be back on the road. The tire inflates . . . but then deflates just as fast. *No, no, no!* I must have nicked my last good tube when popping the tire back on the rim.

No matter, I'll patch it and try again. I pull out my pack of patches and feel around for the glue. A bike bag is a bit like a woman's purse: once something goes in, you can never find it again. I take every last item out of the frame bag. Still no glue. I check the little front pack. Nothing. Somewhere, presumably in Perth, when I packed the bike for the flight to Asia, the glue must have fallen out. With no glue to patch the damaged tube, I am stranded, sixty miles from the nearest town that may or may not have a bike shop.

The sun beats down mercilessly as I sit in the ditch next to the highway, trying to figure out what to do next. My head is aching, and the salty beads of liquid running down my cheeks are not sweat. I feel totally alone. While crying does nothing to resolve my immediate problem, it does at least relieve some of the pent-up frustration. I give in to the moment and let myself blubber. But only for a moment.

Come on, you big baby. Nobody will get you out of this mess except yourself. Where there is a problem, there is always a solution. Think.

I know that Hat Yai is my best option for finding bike parts, and that will mean turning around and going back.

There are few worse things for me than retracing my steps, but I have little choice. I've noticed buses passing by every so often, so I carry Pegasus a few miles south until I find a bus stop on the road. The driver is nice enough to let me on after I show him my flat tire. I awkwardly shove Pegasus between myself and a group of students at the back of the bus. A couple more passengers get on behind me. One has a bundle of paralyzed chickens tied together by the feet, swinging indolently next to the bike wheels. The other is carrying two giant barrels of milk that are almost the same height as himself. It must be market day. Nobody gives me or my bike a second look. Everything and everyone uses the bus in rural Thailand.

After the air and the space of the open road, I feel clammy and claustrophobic in the turbid heat of the packed vehicle. I close my eyes and try to relax. *Breathe in. Breathe out.* I manage to doze.

When the bus finally pulls into Hat Yai, I set off on a fruitless search for a bike shop. Not wanting to destroy the delicate rims, I half-wheel, half-carry Pegasus all around the city. After an hour I'm exhausted. A Thai father, mother, and two daughters are shopping in the market and notice me wandering aimlessly with my bike. They ask what I'm looking for, and I show them the flat tire and the broken spokes.

"Aaahhhh. A moment." One of the teenage daughters says something to her father, who nods and says something back. Then she turns to me. "You come."

"Okay," I say, and follow them.

We don't walk far before they stop in front of a motor-cycle repair shop. The girl takes over once again, explaining the situation to the man inside, who calls his colleague. They look over Pegasus gravely, shaking their heads, comparing motorcycle parts to see if anything matches up to the bicy-cle's tiny parts. The Thai family are starting to get restless. They have shopping to do.

"It's okay if you want to go," I tell the girl. "Thanks for your help. *Cop coon ca.*" I put my hands together and bow my head in a *wai*, the respectful way of saying hello, good-bye, and thank you in Thailand.

She waves goodbye, and I sit down in the shop as the debate continues. One of the mechanics signals, palm out-ward, for me to stay where I am as his partner goes off at a brisk jog, I assume for the necessary parts. I wait for over an hour. Patience may be a virtue, but it's not one of mine. I've already lost half a day and over sixty miles, and I feel myself growing increasingly anxious. But fretting over circum-stances that cannot be changed won't resolve the problem any quicker. *Think of it as a bit of a rest,* I tell myself. I settle into a chair, and someone puts a cold bottle of Coke in my hand.

Eventually the mechanic returns with a fistful of bike nipples of various sizes and a couple of second-hand tubes. I wonder whose bicycle has been dismembered to provide them. Within ten minutes Pegasus's spokes have been fitted with the old/new nipples and the tube has been pumped. I buy some glue and a spare tube.

"*Cop coon maak ca.*" Thank you so much.

The guy shrugs like it's nothing. Bike mechanics are my favorite kind of people.

Today a little kid with a shaved head, wearing a school uniform, nails it when he points me out to his classmates and shouts, "Look! A *phalang*!" The Thai word for "foreigner" is also the local term for "guava," and that's exactly how I feel: pink-faced, with rough, bruised skin and slimy with sweat. Not so much a sophisticated Westerner; more like a feral wild woman. Even after a shower my skin feels grimy, stained brown as much from the dust of the road as from the sun. My fingers look as if they've been dipped in chocolate sauce, as dark tan lines contrast the white of my skin when I take off my gloves. There is a permanent ring of black under the torn fingernails from changing tubes and pumping tires. My two sets of cycling clothes both stink, as they never quite dry overnight. I feel inhuman and unattractive, the furthest thing from female a woman could possibly feel. When clean, fresh-smelling girls pass me in their little dresses, strappy shoes, and shining hair, I feel like a mangy, flea-ridden street dog watching well-groomed thoroughbreds. At these times I long to feel like a woman again. Hell, I'd settle for feeling human!

I stroll back from the 7/11 store with some comfort food—dried fruit, ice cream, and a beer—back to the silence of my hotel room and a fan that barely circulates the stifling warm air. I should be completely used to the solitude by now, but every so often my own company gets old.

When I was a teenager, the realization that I did not belong anywhere was the cause of much self-doubt and grief. I was always a social outsider, a misfit, an observer looking in. The stranger in every group. The only guava in a barrel of apples. Even in a crowd, I could still feel alone. In fact, sometimes that was the loneliest place of all. As an adult, however, I've never been bothered by solitude because I've come to realize that its opposite often means wasting time in the company of people I dislike or with whom I have nothing in common.

"I think solitude is less a conscious choice than an inevitable side-effect of certain life choices," Hendri once told me. If anyone could speak with authority on the merits of solitude, it was he. "When what passes for normal seems the most abnormal thing in the world to pursue, those who decide to go their own way, to be different, to achieve different goals than those society considers 'normal,' will often travel that road alone."

He would tell me that the price of freedom was loneliness. "Freedom to do what you want is a heavy burden to carry and a very lonely road to walk," he wrote in one email. "Freedom is an extreme, because it's by definition selfish. Many search for it, but once they come close enough to grasp the depth and scope of the loneliness they have to cross in order to achieve it, few have the will or desire to take the last committing steps across a barrier of no return for a reward that is not guaranteed."

Hendri understood that there are different kinds of freedom, but the most basic kind is perhaps the most difficult to achieve and the most selfish. "Solo expeditions, mine at least, are the purest form of selfishness I can think of," he told me. "You might not be free from your environment's demands, but you are free to choose your response to them. If a solo mission kills me one day, I won't be the one suffering. It only hurts if you survive. The ones who love me will be left to deal with the sorrow."

It was as if he were predicting his own end with those words. Just a few months later he set off on the expedition through the Congo that would be his last. For those of us who loved him, the loss was devastating.

Now I think about his words, sipping my Chang beer in the silence of the hotel room. I was so angry with him for leaving me behind. There were dark days when I thought about joining him. Endless days dragging by in a lifetime in which he did not exist—that was too abysmal to consider. Setting off to cycle around the world was the only way I knew how to keep on going, to give myself a purpose, a reason for existence. On the bike, I can pound out the emotional pain, and I feel that pain a little less with every mile I travel. Here on the road, all his words have become more real and more relevant to me. Here on the road, I've come close to touching the essence of him. He feels nearer to me now than ever before.

Maybe that is why I've never felt completely alone on this journey.

OCTOBER 19–20, 2012

Traveling as a lone woman, I am usually careful to stick to heavily populated areas as much as possible, especially in developing countries. Today I have decided to break that rule, intent on relaxing and sleeping on the beach. This is the first time I have consciously chosen such an isolated spot to spend the night. I turn off the main road and head toward the coast near Chumphon airport, far from any villages or much civilization. Only after finding a bungalow camp ten yards from the ocean and paying four dollars for a little wooden hut do I discover there's no phone signal. No matter. What could possibly go wrong?

As I finish eating a dinner of green chicken curry on rice, a well-dressed Thai family of four pulls up in an expensive gray jeep. They take the bungalow next to mine, which makes them the only other camp occupants tonight. I relax into a reclining chair on the bamboo porch with a Tiger beer, watching the teenage girls posing for selfies on the beach. A few shaggy mutts that have been frolicking in the sand pad come over for a scratch. They settle on the porch at my feet, and we lie there contentedly as the tide comes in and the sun sinks under the water. The sound of the waves and the gentle evening breeze are powerful sedatives. Growing sleepy, I soon head inside to bed.

It is the dogs' furious barking that wakes me around one a.m. I hear voices and a woman sobbing next door. Through a crack in the curtains, I can see three men out-

side the family's bungalow. The father is standing at the
open door in his pajamas, and one of the men roughly pulls
him out. I recognize two of them from earlier in the evening: they were eating at a nearby table and watched me
ride up, dusty and disheveled. They left about the same
time the family arrived.

Something about the developing scene seems very
wrong—and very familiar. My body begins to shake vio-
lently, and a terrible heat rises from the pit of my stomach up
to my chest. I'm immediately back in Uganda, where I had
gone to help my father start a radio show. At twenty-one
years old, I'm tied up next to several of my youngest siblings
with an AK-47 pressed to my temple. My father is being held
down while our assailants threaten to hack his foot off with
a machete if we don't give them money. The terrifying ordeal
goes on for three hours. For the next two weeks, every noise
would wake me. Every footstep in the hall would send my
body into a fit of post-traumatic convulsions. The memories
have mercifully faded over time. Until tonight.

With the latent trauma reawakened, panic rapidly takes
over reason. My body trembles, and bile burns a path from
my stomach to my throat. I fight to reassert control over my
body. I remember something I read once about fear having
either of two meanings: "forget everything and run" or "face
everything and rise." The choice is mine.

Mind over matter. Calm down. Think. Nothing has happened to me yet. If they come to my door, what can they do?
They would have to break down the door to enter. What
could they take from me? I have nothing except my bike.

They saw me roll in, so they must guess I have very little money.

I sit down on the bed, considerably calmer, my body no longer shaking. I'm also thinking more clearly. Are the emergency services 911 or 999 in Thailand? It doesn't matter. Even if I knew which number to call, there's no phone signal. And even if I could contact someone, I don't know the name of the road or the campsite. I turn on my GPS, but it fails to pick up a satellite signal, so its emergency button is useless. If something were to happen to me out here, I suddenly realize, no one would ever know.

I lean back on the pillow, alert to the slightest sound outside, and have a long think. After running through every potential outcome and exhausting every possibility, I arrive at the last and worst-case scenario. Death. There have been times during the ride when I have thought that I wouldn't care if I died just then, in a place I want to be, doing what I most want to do. In those moments, I hardly cared if I'd finish the journey. Dying did not scare me; it was living without feeling alive that was frightening.

Now, though, the farther I get, the more I find myself wanting to reach the finish line, wanting to see more, do more, experience more. Life has become far more attractive—not living merely for the sake of existing, but honoring the fact that I exist by really living.

"Have you read much of Osho?" Hendri asked me once during one of our Skype chats.

We liked to discuss the books and authors we were reading. Hendri's wanderings started to take an internal direction toward the end of his life, and the philosophies of various gurus often reflected that. He liked to bounce their ideas off me. He said I had a way of keeping him from wandering too far. Our conversation that night had veered toward death, with Hendri explaining that he viewed dying as the ultimate adventure from which there was no return, like a one-way ticket to Mars. He talked about it as if he couldn't wait.

"To the man who has not known what life is, death is an enemy; and to the man who knows what life is, death is the ultimate crescendo of life." Osho's words—in Hendri's voice—come to me now, as I'm lying in the darkness, listening for footsteps approaching my door. Ending up with death as the final scenario feels strangely comforting, like the thought of a soft pillow when you're tired. If there is no consciousness after death, then once I'm dead, I won't be aware that I ever existed. And if there is consciousness, well, fresh adventure take me!

Tomorrow I'll have to wake up early and pedal. And if something happens between now and then, it will happen. Sitting up and waiting for it won't change a thing. I pull the sheet over my shoulders, shut my eyes, and sleep.

OCTOBER 20, 2012

Just like every other day, I awake at dawn. All is silent as I pull on my shorts, load up my bags, and wheel Pegasus outside. I look about cautiously; there is no movement from my neighbors' hut. Did I imagine the whole thing? No police have turned up; there was no further commotion; the family's car is still parked in the driveway. Perhaps my imagination ran away with me last night. How much of it was real? How much did my mind create?

The three dogs are still sprawled across my porch, directly in front of the door. My mangy guardians stretch and wag their tails when I emerge, nuzzling their noses against my legs. "What good doggies you are." I reward them with belly rubs, while the expressive mutts whine, lick my hands, and fight each other for my affection.

With a strong feeling of relief, I pedal back on to a busy road.

The feeling is short-lived. A couple hours later I realize I'm being followed by a motorcyclist on a red scooter. He stays a few yards behind me for a few minutes, then overtakes me and rides a few yards ahead, then pulls over to the side of the road and waits until I pass, then shadows me once more. As per my usual tactic, I plug earphones into my ears and pretend not to notice him, while keeping an eye out from behind the dark lenses of my sunglasses.

He grows bolder as time passes, coming right up next to me and launching into an impressive repertoire of dirty words. I decide it's time to go on the offensive, so I whip out my phone and start snapping his picture. This appears to rattle him. He speeds up and turns off the highway at a sharp bend in the road. The moment he's out of sight, I swerve onto a side road and head into a service station toilet, where

I hunker down with Pegasus for a good twenty minutes until I feel it's safe to emerge again.

The events of last night and today have compounded my feeling of being completely alone and vulnerable. The animal without a pack is an animal without protection. It's little wonder humans always search for a group to which they might belong. We have a subconscious need to attach ourselves to a pack for safety, passed down through evolutionary millennia. Nobody wants to be the solitary animal.

OCTOBER 22, 2012

A classic red convertible with painted flames licking up the sides and a deafening engine pulls up outside the 7/11 where I'm getting breakfast and stocking up on snacks. A minute later four Thai men dressed in leather and lots of silver pile through the door. I love Thai service station stops. They have everything from fresh sliced fruit served with a salt, sugar, and chili dip to green tea milkshakes, crunchy wasabi peas, and endless varieties of dried fruit. The salty mango and papaya are my favorites. I carry plastic bags of dried fruit in my little handlebar bag and suck on pieces throughout the day to make the long hours in the saddle less tedious.

Outside the 7/11 a number of market stalls are selling hot and spicy street food, sarongs, car tools, and random paraphernalia. One aging vendor is sitting behind a table on which is a rather impressive display of knives, swords, and switchblades. I used to have a sword collection, so I stroll over for a closer look. One of the elaborately costumed gang members also sashays over to the stand with his best *I'm a badass cowboy* swagger. He's dressed in a skin-tight black tank top, tasseled leather trousers decorated with a large silver buckle and chains, and a giant silver and turquoise medallion around his neck. His long, multibraided hair is partially covered by a faux-aged leather cowboy hat. He evidently feels that dressing up as his anime-themed alter ego is cool, and subsequently so do I. The manga cowboy picks up two of the Japanese katanas and begins dancing with them, whirling the swords in coordinated movements, slashing the air closer and closer to where I'm standing. He's showing off. He knows it; I know it.

"*Gang mak!*" I say with a thumbs-up, and receive the shy smile of a schoolboy getting some much-desired approval from his teacher. Not such a tough guy after all. "Photo?" I ask, holding up my phone.

He grabs it from my hand eagerly, passes it to the old man behind the stand, says something in Thai, and receives a nod in reply. A sword still in each hand, he breaks into a range of practiced poses next to me until his friends whistle that they're ready to leave.

"You. Very cool," he tells me.

"You very cool too," I say.

He seems pleased to hear it and gives my hand a vigorous shake. His friends are already in the convertible, revving the engine ostentatiously, and he jumps into the backseat without opening the door. The four of them salute me with fists raised in the air, shouting "Cool bike, *phalang*," as they roar away, leaving me much gratified by the validation.

I continue another thirty-five miles down the road. At around midday, the hottest time of day, I decide to find somewhere to break for lunch. Bangkok is now no more than forty miles away, and I've booked a flight to India for the following morning, so I can afford to rest for an hour or two. A jeep has pulled off the road, and I stop to ask how far it is to the nearest village. The family of three sisters and one brother, ranging in age from twenty to fifty, don't speak much English, so I signal by raising my fingers to my mouth.

"*Gin ahaan*," I say. Eat food.

"Aaaaahhh," the sisters say simultaneously, then chatter together for a minute.

"You eat shrimp?" the youngest finally asks. She is clearly the designated translator, having learned some basic English in school.

"*Dai ka!*" Of course I do.

"*Koon gin kap rea.*" You eat with us. "Eat shrimp, okay?"

"Okay."

She signals for me to follow them. They pile back into the jeep and crawl down the road for a couple of miles while I follow behind as fast as I can. After ten minutes they pull up next to a makeshift structure with bamboo and straw thatching that serves as an open-air restaurant. Rustic tables and benches are scattered around on the uneven bare earth. Three massive plastic tubs are off to one side of the seating area, filled with water and giant tiger prawns. Customers get up and scoop out bucketfuls of live shrimp—as much as they want to eat—and hand them to the cook to roast or fry.

For the next hour, we eat fried shrimp and drink Singha beer till we can eat and drink no more. Through a combination of my limited Thai, their limited English, and a whole lot of sign language and sound effects, they hear all about my adventures, and I learn all about their lives and jobs. They're a close family of independent women, all either working or studying, all now single, with one a single mother and one divorced.

"No men," they say with two thumbs down. "Men *mai ben*." No good. The brother, who is the oldest of the four siblings and married, just smiles and shrugs. How can you fight a family of feisty women?

We part knowing we'll never see each other again but glad we met for lunch. It's one of those unplanned moments that you sometimes get on a journey, when a memory you will never forget is created like a photograph or a postcard. They were on a family day out together, yet for an hour they invited me, a complete stranger, into their world.

Revolving day by day within our tiny individual worlds, it's easy to get an inflated sense of self and see the world from an egocentric perspective. Being the outsider in other people's worlds makes me realize what an insignificant cog I am in this larger machine called humanity. The more you travel, the smaller the world becomes, while at the same time you and the things you thought were important shrink, too.

I continue pedaling toward Bangkok, belly bloated and gurgling with too much half-digested shrimp, head woozy from too many beers, but it's worth it.

Bangkok is a daunting metropolis that is a nightmare for cyclists. It takes as long to cross the city and reach the airport as it took to cycle the previous thirty miles. The most harrowing part of the whole ordeal is the final airport approach. I cannot find any small back roads, so I'm left with no choice but to pedal along the highway. Cars honk as they speed by at sixty miles per hour. I hug the curb of the overpass, as close as I can get to the metal barrier. It's terrifying and seems to go on for ever. When I finally ride into the airport complex, tense and shaken, stomach churning, I could kiss the tarmac.

INDIAN NIGHTMARES

My first day cycling in India starts with a bang. Trying to get out of Kolkata, I weave through the seething, living chaos of trucks, buses, rickshaws, and bikes laden with pots, animals, and merchandise; of pedestrians, motorists, other cyclists, dogs, cows, goats, and piles of garbage, and everywhere there is an interminable stench of rotting rubbish, feces, and sickly sweet incense.

A truck approaches on my right, and I'm already hugging the curb when a man darts out into the street, directly in my path. He sees me two feet away and freezes. There's nowhere to swerve to avoid him, and it's far too late to brake. "Move! Move! *Move!*" I shout, milliseconds before impact. The collision sends Pegasus and me sprawling across the pavement.

"Are you crazy?" I yell at no one. The guy has already scampered away. I pick myself up and realign the bike chain.

"People with a death wish . . ." I mutter testily, ignoring the blood dripping down my shin and shakily remounting Pegasus. I just want to get onto the open road, but it takes over two hours to maneuver my way out of the city.

Twenty-five miles down the highway, my stomach reminds me I haven't eaten breakfast. At a little roadside truck stop restaurant, I pull over for chai and biscuits. While I eat, a small crowd gathers around Pegasus, pinching and prodding the tires as if they were testing fruit for ripeness. "Expensive?" they ask in the international sign language for money, rubbing thumb and first two fingers together.

"No, noooo," I lie, vigorously shaking my head.

Pegasus is a two-wheel rock star around here. Each time I stop along the road from Kolkata to Bhubaneshwar, a new crowd swoops in. At first this makes me nervous and claustrophobic, but gradually I begin to understand that most of the attention is focused on the bicycle. People gather just to touch the tires; they have never seen any so thin. Even covered in dust and filth, compared to the rusty single-gear contraptions they all ride, Pegasus sticks out like a Ferrari next to tractors. One more reason not to let my bike out of my sight. I squeeze into the toilet cubicles with him, and he is always within arm's reach wherever I stop to eat.

After eighty miles I'm getting desperately hungry and thirsty and feeling the effects of the sun. I ride into Kharagpur, where throngs of men with orange powder smeared down the centers of their foreheads are blocking the road and waving three-foot-long sabers to the rhythm of drums.

It's the national Hindu festival of Dussehra, which celebrates the Lord Rama's victory over the demon king Ramaha—the age-old triumph of good over evil.

I had no idea before flying into India that I would be arriving on a public holiday. Everything is closed, apart from a few filthy roadside stalls cooking food next to piles of rubbish that are pecked by crows and sniffed by cadaverous street dogs. Everything—rubbish, food, and scavengers—is covered with flies. Having lived in Mumbai as a child, I know better than to eat food from street stalls. You should only ever drink bottled water and eat packaged food or fresh food that is cooked in front of you. I remember that we soaked all the vegetables and fruit from the market in salt water for at least an hour. My stomach may be tougher than most, but nobody passes through India unscathed. I can only hope I developed some kind of immunity to the worst of the bacteria during childhood.

When I finally find a restaurant that seems to be open, they tell me they won't be serving food until the evening.

"Please," I beg, "I'm so hungry, I'll eat anything you've got."

I must look especially pathetic, because they take pity on me and offer some leftover biryani. I figure as long as they heat the food over a fire, it should be all right. There is no real alternative. I scarf down the fragrant yellow rice while the owner, cook, and waiter sit on a row of plastic chairs to watch me. The waiter keeps trying to persuade me to take him to "my country" so he can get a visa. I try to explain that there is no "my country," but eventually give up in favor of stuffing my face.

Fed and watered, I ask for the toilet and am escorted into a dark, cavernous room full of rubbish and dirty pots. From the industrial stove in the center, I deduce that this is also the kitchen. The waiter points to an open drain in the corner: "There."

I realize with mounting horror that they must have cooked the food I have just eaten in here.

"Never mind," I say, smiling weakly, and briefly consider retching up my lunch.

Meanwhile the owner has mounted Pegasus and is taking a wobbly spin around the little cement courtyard. I let out a nervous yelp when he nearly crashes into a wall. It's definitely time to go.

"Uh, thank you for the food," I say. "I must be leaving now." With one possessive hand on Pegasus's handlebars, I pay for lunch, wondering what the fate of my stomach will be and knowing from experience that an internal war against the sudden germ invasion has already begun.

Cycling out of town toward the highway, I am pursued by a couple of young men on a motorbike. They are dressed like Bollywood sidekicks: collared shirts buttoned low, rolled up at the sleeves, and tucked into tight jeans; hair extravagantly gelled; aviator sunglasses. "Madam, stop a moment!" they holler at me.

I refuse to stop, but they follow persistently for a few miles.

"Please, madam, we just want to take photos with you."

When it becomes clear that they aren't going to leave me alone, I pull over. A second motorbike with two more guys on board putters alongside. The four of them jump off their bikes and take turns posing next to me, with the enthusiastic photographer of the group commenting between snaps, "Oh, yes, very sexy." Yeah, right. That is exactly how I would describe myself right now.

Eventually I get rid of them and am back on the road. The sun starts setting at four, and by five it is almost dark. I decide to turn off at the little town of Belda. I am not about to cycle alone at night in India. There is only one hotel—on the second floor of a crumbling building with peeling pink paint—where a vociferous argument is taking place between the manager and a cross-eyed old woman. They are too absorbed in the heated exchange to notice me enter. A huddle of mustachioed men are sitting on the single lobby sofa, listening, laughing, and commenting on the uproar. I wait a good twenty minutes until it becomes clear that acquiring fresh clientele is less of a priority than winning the debate. Eventually I plant myself impatiently in front of the manager's desk, so it's impossible for him to ignore me. He stares up with a distinctly hostile look that says I have no business standing there.

"Hello, I need a room."

"How many in your party?" Apparently I have an invisible entourage.

"Just me."

"You are alone?" He looks at me incredulously, uncertain how to proceed.

One of the guys from the peanut gallery says something in Hindi, with a single discernible word—"cycle." The manager glances from me to Pegasus, then back to me, and starts laughing as though this is the most ridiculous thing he's ever heard. Shaking his head and mumbling something under his breath, he puts me through the laborious registration formalities, and I'm finally led to a room with yellowing walls, a bare straw mattress, a clothesline slung from wall to wall, and no toilet paper or soap. I plod back wearily to the front desk and act out the motions of putting a sheet on the bed. The manager rolls his eyes and calls the assistant, who reluctantly drags himself over.

Meanwhile the cross-eyed woman has dashed to the linen cupboard, pulled out some bedding, and rushed into my room. Leaping nimbly onto the bed, she throws out the sheet like a fisherman casting a net. The assistant, roused by the activity, follows a few seconds behind and tears off the freshly laid sheet with a single violent movement. This sets off a volley of unintelligible expletives from the woman, which the assistant fires back just as rapidly, before chasing her from the room with one hand raised threateningly. She continues her screeching tirade in the hall, while he slowly and methodically makes up the bed again. Although I cannot understand a word, the whole drama is incredibly entertaining.

When they finally leave me alone, I turn to lock the door

and discover there is no key. So it is back to the front desk again. The manager pretends not to understand. I mime a key being turned in a lock. He shrugs and waves a hand as if to say *Don't worry about it*. I'm plenty worried about it, of course, and insist that I must have a key and cannot sleep the night with an unlocked door. He reluctantly pulls open a drawer and hands one over.

Returning to my room, I nearly collide with the old woman, who is waiting for me with one hand outstretched and the other pointing to her open palm. I ignore her and close and lock the door, vaguely wondering what will await me when I open it in the morning.

OCTOBER 25, 2012

At six a.m. I am awakened by the sound of the doorknob slowly turning. When whoever is on the other side finds it locked, they start pounding their fists against it instead. I unlock the door and pull it open with some displeasure, to find the persistent old woman standing there, still pointing to her palm. I imagine the argument of the previous night probably had something to do with her disturbing the clientele with her entrepreneurial tip-seeking.

It is an inauspicious start to my second day in India, which soon takes a flying nosedive. The biryani of the day before has already taken effect. I awoke in the middle of the night, my stomach an internal tsunami, and spent most of the next few hours on the toilet. I know I risk severe dehy-dration by cycling in the Indian heat without food in my stomach, but I am not prepared to stay another day in this hotel of horrors, so I pack up my gear and aim to reach Balasore, sixty miles away. They prove to be the longest sixty miles I have ever cycled. My head is pounding and my stomach is close to imploding—or exploding—before I have even left Belda.

Antonio calls around ten-thirty. "Everything okay?"

"No. I don't know if I can go on. I have to go to the toilet so badly I can hardly pedal."

"So just stop somewhere."

The sound that comes gurgling out of me is somewhere between a cry of pain and a hysterical laugh. "*Just stop—where?* I'm on a highway in the middle of nowhere."

"Listen, I'll book into a hotel in Balasore and see if they can come and get you."

I keep on pedaling, dizzy from the heat and from the unbearable pain in my gut.

Antonio calls again. "Ju, you're booked into a clean hotel. Just try to reach Balasore, and then you can rest."

I wonder what planet he's on. A lot of sarcastic replies come to mind, but "'Kay" is all I can manage to say before hanging up.

I have to stop every few miles, with one leg wrapped tightly around the other like a licorice stick while my stom-ach rumbles and shakes with the early stirrings of yet another intestinal eruption. By the time I enter Balasore, there is no more holding it. Right in the middle of the street, it explodes, and I run with crossed legs into the first hotel I see. "Help!" I shout desperately. "Please! The toilet!"

The old white-bearded man in a turban at the reception desk points wordlessly to a door at the end of the hall. The next half hour is pretty gross and grim. Fortunately there is a shower in the bathroom, and I use it to wash myself, my clothes, and lastly the room itself. As I rinse out my soiled shorts, I start laughing. It is one of those scenarios you hear about but never imagine could happen to you. I have crapped myself like a baby at thirty-one years of age. I think I may have hit my lowest point yet. Veritable rock bottom. It can't get any worse than this, can it? Putting my wet clothes back on, I emerge from the bathroom feeling sheepish.

"Thank you," I mumble to the man behind the desk.

"Ten rupees." With that, he declares the extent of his indifference. I fish out the cost of my shame and slink out, all pride completely pulverized.

The hotel Antonio has booked me into is six miles farther up the road. The luxury of a clean bed has never been more appreciated, and I stay in it for the remainder of the day. I hope the rest will allow me to start pedaling again tomorrow morning.

OCTOBER 26, 2012

Keeping down some yogurt and boiled eggs for breakfast is all the encouragement I need to get going. Antonio calls and advises me to rest an extra day, but I'm up and back on the road by seven-thirty. Over 125 miles later, I reach the city of Bhubaneshwar, running a high fever.

OCTOBER 27, 2012

One day my stubbornness will be the death of me. This morning I cannot get out of bed. As much as it kills me to admit it, if I don't stop and rest now, I risk being laid up for days with something serious. The obvious solution is a course of antibiotics and lots of sleep.

The threat of India has hung as heavy as a black cloud over my entire journey. Before I started, I was well aware of the variety of difficulties I could expect to encounter, including sickness. The years I lived in Thailand and the time I spent in India were like day and night. It was my father who loved India. He dragged his first wife and two kids to the subcontinent, where he launched his first successful radio show, had a third kid, and then abandoned them there. A few years later, when I was eight, he dragged me to India, deposited me in the cult's boarding school, and left me there while he went off to pursue his latest love affair in another commune.

I remember doing exercises in the courtyard with twenty other children one afternoon when the doorbell suddenly rang. One of our teachers went to the gate to see who it was, spoke briefly with whoever was on the other side, and came back shaking his head and laughing. "A rich Indian couple," he told the other teacher. "They thought this was an orphanage and wanted to adopt one of the children." All I could think was *Take me! Please take me!* By then it had been so long since I had seen my mother and so rarely did I see my father that I truly felt I was an orphan.

The next time my father packed me off to India, I was an angry, disappointed thirteen-year-old who had committed the unthinkable crime of saying I wanted to leave the Children of God. His solution was to send me away for "retraining," in a bid to break my rebellious spirit. I fell desperately ill with fever and diarrhea not long after arriving at the commune in Mumbai. Since the cult believed physical ailments had a direct connection to spiritual malady, they took my illness as a sure sign that I needed curing and proceeded to go about it as soon as I could eat again. After many confessions and exorcisms, I was put on permanent enforced silence. I was made to clean, cook, and wander the streets under the relentless sun for ten hours a day, selling the cult's tapes, videos, and literature. I left four months later, angrier and more rebellious than ever.

Perhaps these memories have tainted my perception of India, but of all the countries I lived in throughout my childhood, it is the only one I never wanted to visit again. To me, it has always been a place of unnecessary filth, disease, and ignorance, overwhelming stench, great disparity between the castes, and misogyny that manifests itself most alarmingly in the high rape statistics. A place where human life holds less value than that of cows, which are deified. When people I meet in Europe sigh and use terms such as "deep" and "spiritual" when describing their life-changing journeys through the country, I remain silent. I cannot believe that true spiritual enlightenment would ever include such dismal side-effects.

It has been only four days, and my deeply pessimistic expectations for this part of my trip have already been exceeded. With another ten days to go before I reach Mumbai, I shudder to think what else might possibly go wrong.

OCTOBER 28, 2012

Though I'm still weak, the course of antibiotics I packed in my medicine bag has worked miracles. The fever burned itself out during the night, and since resting a second day is not an option, I pack up and leave Bhubaneshwar, heading southwest toward Brahmapur.

Cycling alone through India is nerve-racking in itself. Never mind the heat, the chaotic traffic, the potholes, and the sickness. My bike draws attention. As a lone foreign woman, I draw attention. As a lone foreign woman riding a bicycle, Pegasus and I draw crowds of circus-freak-show proportions. Every time I stop, be it in the middle of a town or the middle of nowhere, within seconds I'm mobbed by hordes of silent, staring men. It's disquieting at best. In one town where I stop for lunch, the mob around me grows so thick I can't move, and the police have to break through with batons to disperse them.

Today, sick, hot, tired, and surrounded by yet another jostling mob, I finally snap. I need directions to the next town, and nobody will answer my persistent inquiries. All they do is stare until the tension in the air is palpable. Hemmed in on all sides, with the crowd pushing against me and Pegasus, I feel as panicky as a caged animal. My response is to start acting like one. I shout and wave my arms around in a fairly accurate imitation of a crazy monkey. No one can understand what I'm saying, but I can see the surprise and uncertainty on their faces. I push my bike through the horde, and they part for me to pass. Nobody follows.

For the second time in my journey, I feel extremely unsafe. Even while pedaling, I am often followed for dozens of miles by men on motorcycles. At first I tried to ignore them completely, putting my earphones into my ears and pretending I couldn't hear their rude remarks. This hardly deterred them though; in fact, it appeared to spur them on. Finally I realized that it works better to act aggressive, so now I shout loudly and even maniacally, threatening motorbike stalkers with a raised fist. First they laugh, but then they look worried and eventually ride off as my gestures inevitably attract the curiosity of bystanders and passing motorists. Acting big and bold can attract the wrong kind of attention, but when used at the right times, it can be a highly effective weapon in a lone female's arsenal.

Antonio hears my anxiety whenever he calls—as long as I pick up. Often I don't answer, as replying would mean stopping, something I try to avoid at all costs, especially in highly populated areas. Flashing my iPhone to an audience would be reckless. Naturally he is becoming concerned.

"Ju, Nicola is coming down there to find you," he tells me when I finally pull over to answer one call. "Wait till he arrives." Nicola is a mutual friend from Naples, a jack-of-all-trades who is useful to have around in just about any situation.

"What? No. I'm okay, really."

"You are not okay. This is the first time I've ever heard you so nervous over the phone. Nicola will follow you for the next week. He can reach you in a couple of days."

"I'm not waiting for a couple of days. I'll keep going."

"Okay. But stop if you feel unsafe."

Unsafe or not, stopping is not an option. Never.

NOVEMBER 2, 2012

It's three days before Nicola finds me on the road. His car has had more flats than my bike. The poor guy has never been to India before, or to any other developing country for that matter. He's more shaken than I am when he finally reaches me, and he hugs me like a drowning man clinging to a life raft. I suspect he's never been more happy to see a familiar face.

"I don't know how you are cycling here!" he comments in Italian. "Just driving on these roads is traumatizing. I know I don't speak English very well, but nobody understands *anything* I say here. They all just nod their heads like they understand, then do the opposite."

I have to laugh. The physical discomforts of grime, hunger, and sickness are easier to endure when you can joke about them with someone else. I've grown used to managing alone, but having Nicola nearby for a few days will help take the edge off this Indian ordeal, at least mentally. Physically it's not getting any easier.

A typhoon has just hit my route down the southeast coast toward Chennai. The strong winds and heavy rain are making it difficult to see the road, especially the potholes. After changing another burst tube, I continue more cautiously, which slows my progress considerably, but at least the bad weather means there are fewer people and motorcycles on the road.

I wrap my saddlebag in multiple plastic bags in an attempt to keep out the wet, but by the time I stop for the day, everything is drenched and covered in mud and human excrement. The concept of public toilets has not yet caught on in most of India. Morning and evening, villagers simply squat along the main road with a bucket of water to do their business. This, mixed with mud and garbage, more or less covers Pegasus and me from head to toe at the end of every day. It takes more than an hour to clean myself and the bike, and the shower floor is covered with a thick layer of muck by the time I've finished. Nothing is ever dry by the morning, but that hardly matters, since everything will be soaked again long before midday.

As a result of all this, my clothes and gear have begun to stink terribly. My immune system is weak from the incessant diarrhea and bad nutrition. My stomach cannot handle the heavy spices of the local food, and it's almost impossible to find anything plain. I am eating less each day and losing weight. I have picked up a chest infection, and my throat is sore from the constant wet and wind. In short, I am feeling pretty miserable right now.

It always seems worst at night, at the end of a long day on the road, failing to find food I can keep down, watching roaches climbing up the walls of my four-dollar-a-night hotel room. Morning always brings fresh courage. I steel my mind and tell myself everything is temporary. This is a test of endurance, and it's true what they say: you're always stronger than you think. I have gotten this far. What is another week, or even another couple of months?

I embarked on this journey knowing there would be moments when I would question the whole thing and my motives for doing it, when I would think the hardship and struggle outweighed the good times. The Facebook updates show only the highlights—exciting snapshots of interesting or beautiful moments. But cycling the world also involves long periods of tedium, exhaustion, and dealing with recurring problems daily.

Every great challenge changes you in some way. Without the usual comfort and safety of a familiar environment, the support of family and friends, I can rely on no one and nothing but myself. Forced to tap into my own inner reserves of strength, I am finding out what I am capable of enduring, both physically and mentally.

NOVEMBER 5, 2012

The typhoon is showing no signs of letting up, so Antonio suggests cutting my route down the coast to Chennai and heading inland toward Hyderabad instead. After four days of continuous rain, the sun is finally breaking through the clouds. I can certainly benefit from some drying out.

The middle of southern India is less populated, with beautiful, verdant countryside. Farmers drive herds of cows, with their horns painted in bright blues and oranges. Groups of women in colorful saris chat and laugh as they stroll down the dusty roads, children in tow. Everyone seems less aggressive. I get more smiles and waves, and fewer crowds mobbing me. I am starting to relax and enjoy the ride.

The farther west I go, the more Western the population becomes in terms of both behavior and dress. I come upon the first McDonald's I have seen since arriving in India, and while I'm normally that franchise's greatest detractor, for once I'm actually glad to see the giant yellow M towering above the smog. Hopeful I will find some food that isn't drowned in spices, I park Pegasus against the window, next to a life-size Ronald McDonald with a red goatee, so I can keep an eye on him from inside.

The restaurant has air-conditioning and free wi-fi.

Groups of wealthy teenagers are gossiping, ribbing each other, and generally making a ruckus. Girls dressed in pastel-colored salwar kameezes, thickly braided hair looped around their ears or hanging past their waists, are sipping milk-shakes, giggling, and teasing the downy-faced youths at a nearby table. It could be an after-school scene anywhere in the world, but after ten days of dilapidated cities and rural villages steeped in abject poverty, the contrast is jarring.

I order a chicken burger, which comes marinated in chil-ies and spices. Hope deferred. I guess even McDonald's is adaptable. No matter. Much of the world lives on plain rice, and so can I.

NOVEMBER 8, 2012

Mumbai airport at last! The final challenge is to find—or fashion—a bike box for Pegasus. Unlike every other country I have visited, people don't simply dispose of boxes in India, so I am unlikely to find a free one. In the end I stumble across a shop in the slums near the airport that sells secondhand cardboard boxes. The dirty walls of the small room are cov-ered from floor to ceiling with stacks of flattened ones. I buy ten of the biggest and from them construct one giant box with the help of three rolls of packing tape. It's not pretty, but it doesn't need to be. It just has to hold together for the length of the flight—over Pakistan, Afghanistan, and Iran (three countries I could not pass through as a lone woman) and on to Turkey.

Nicola will be flying back to Italy tomorrow, so we have a last dinner of barbecued meat together before parting company. "*In bocca al lupo*." He kisses me on both cheeks and gives me a hug. "See you back in Napoli soon."

A long line of passengers are waiting to enter the airport. To get into the building, we all have to show our passports and our tickets. I flash the electronic ticket on my smartphone and am told this is unacceptable. Apparently I have to present a printout.

"Sorry, but how do I get my flight?" I ask the surly official who is barking orders at other frustrated passengers.

"Madam, you must wait till the check-in opens. Then someone from the airline will print your ticket and escort you inside."

I was hoping to catch a bit of sleep on a row of chairs somewhere inside the building. It's eleven-thirty p.m. Check-in for my flight won't open for another two hours.

"So what do I do now?" My irritation closely mirrors the official's.

"Go to the waiting lounge," he orders me.

"Great. Where's that?"

"At the end of the building, past all the entrances."

I follow his instructions and wheel the mummified Pegasus to the very end of the terminal. The waiting lounge turns out to be simply where the road ends. People and their trolleys, piled high with luggage, litter the pavement. So much for my hopes of a comfy seat. I'm still in India, lest I forget. It isn't over till it's over. I find an empty patch of pavement and sit against the wall to wait with everyone else. A couple in front of me picnics on a dal and chapatti dinner. Families socialize. Chai wallahs circulate with hot pots of sweet spiced tea. Groups of soldiers pass back and forth with sniffer dogs on leashes.

I doze with one hand, as always, on my bike.

TURKISH DELIGHTS

Smooth riding welcome! Good, cheap food in giant portions welcome! Turkey welcome! In my first day here, the Turkish people have been so welcoming and so far removed from the comments posted on Facebook by friends and followers who are concerned for my safety. I'm baffled why anyone would think that women cannot travel safely on their own in Turkey.

I landed at a rainy Ankara airport yesterday afternoon and decided to spend the night at a nearby hotel and make an early start this morning. It's still pouring buckets when I get up at seven a.m., but that is hardly an excuse to stay in bed, and wishing it were won't make it so.

I lost four and a half pounds in India, and I'm feeling as emaciated as I look. To make up for two weeks of culinary deprivation, I go food crazy. The hotel breakfast is an unexpected delight: soup, a platter of cheese, fresh vegetables, olives, hummus, eggs and pickles, honey, and hot bread. Turkey shares its Mediterranean neighbors' climate, which must contribute to the excellence of the food. The tomatoes are sweet, the olives large and fleshy, the fresh herbs abundant, and the variety of goat cheese extensive. I am tempted to stop at every chance to eat again.

The cold and rain make riding difficult. The roads are turning into rivers, and it is impossible to see the potholes. I hit a huge drain hole riding out of Ankara. Both my water bottles go flying into the speeding traffic, and it is impossible to retrieve them. It is a small miracle my front rim hasn't buckled. A purple lump soon balloons where my shin smashed against the pedal. By the time I reach the southern outskirts of the city, I am drenched; the cold has crept deep into my core, and my insides are like ice. There is only one thing to do—beat a retreat to the nearest restaurant for a second breakfast.

I pull off my dripping gloves, pop them onto a nearby heater to dry, and head to the bathroom to change my wet socks. A strange burning smell greets me when I return to the table; smoke is funneling up from under my gloves. The waiter notices it too and points frantically to the heater. I tear them off quickly, but the damage has been done. My gloves have been burned to a crisp, with giant holes splitting the fabric. *Great going, Juliana. Real clever.*

No use crying over spilt milk. A tasty spread in a toasty restaurant makes the loss of my gloves easier to swallow. It also makes it that much harder to leave. I drag myself— inwardly kicking and screaming—back into the wind and rain. As Hendri used to say whenever he was suffering through a particularly difficult day on an expedition, "Make it harder!"

Unlike the Turkish people, Turkish dogs are decidedly unfriendly. Let me rephrase that: they are terror-inspiring lions with big jaws and even bigger appetites. I look over my shoulder to see a pack of fifteen of the massive, white, wild variety heading straight toward me from half a mile away, racing up the hill, fangs bared and hungry.

"Fuuuuu . . ." I cry in panic, before all I can manage is desperate, heavy breathing.

There is nothing like a dog chase to pump the adrenaline. Pedaling uphill in frantic fear of life and limb, I feel like a hunted rabbit with an exploding heart. I have no doubt that the dogs see me as nothing more than a giant steak on wheels. They close in with strategic wolf-pack coordination. Some run on ahead, presumably with the intention of grabbing my front wheel; the rest circle on all sides. Death by dog is not how I imagined I would go. *Keep pedaling, goddammit!*

At that moment a loud horn blasts close behind me, and I turn to see a car racing down the middle of the pack. One dog squeals as the car crunches into it, and the rest leap out of the way. I pedal into the center of the road, and the driver pulls up alongside, effectively creating a barrier

between me and the dogs. He keeps his hand on the horn
the entire time. The dogs continue to bark and snap. I
crest the hill, accelerate to a heady speed on the descent,
and watch the pack fall back as they realize the chase is
futile. I will live to cycle another day. The driver waves
and drives on. I give him a thumbs-up. Thank God for
road angels.

Still rattled by my narrow escape, I stop for a late lunch
at a little restaurant next to a roadside service station. The
owner and his son seem pleased when I shuffle through the
door. As their only customer, they roll out the royal treatment. Naturally they are curious to know what I am doing
out here, alone on a bike, so I tell them all about the world
cycle. We understand each other perfectly, even though the
whole conversation is conducted in charades, since they
speak no more than five words of English and I know even
less Turkish. I'm grateful for my years in Italy, where com-
munication with the hands is part of everyday life.

They want to know what I think of Turkey.

Food, superb. People, wonderful. But as for the dogs! Let
me tell you about the dogs! I gesticulate my latest misadven-
ture, ending with the motorist scattering the pack with his
car. Apparently this is one of the funniest things they've ever
heard. They pound the table as they laugh.

"It wasn't funny at the time, trust me," I say.

They suggest that I must be very hungry after a chase like
that.

"Yes, very. What is good to eat?" I point at something on
the menu.

They give an approving thumbs-up and manage to find the English words "Good meat."

"What kind of meat is it?"

They look perplexed, so it's back to the old charades, along with some sound effects.

"Moooo?" I suggest, making horns with my fingers.

They shake their heads.

I do the funky chicken, clucking moronically.

More head-shaking.

"Baaaa?"

"Yes! Yes!"

A few minutes later I'm enjoying a rich lamb stew, chunky bread, and lots of cheese.

Language is overrated.

NOVEMBER 14, 2012

The terrain through the middle of Turkey is arid, with long, gradual climbs and descents. It can get a bit monotonous, but at least there are frequent service stations along the highways for breaks. Whenever I stop at a station, I find one of the staff waiting for me outside the toilets with a cup of scalding-hot Turkish tea. This keeps me well hydrated. Maybe too hydrated. I then have to stop at the next station to use their toilet. Once again tea is offered, I drink the tea . . . and on it goes.

My tires are wearing thin. I last changed them just before the Nullarbor in Australia and have pedaled some 4,040 miles since. I'm unlikely to find a bike shop before Istanbul, so I've been riding on a prayer, hoping nothing too dramatic happens between now and then. Worn tires mean more punctures. I had one yesterday and this morning I awoke to another flat tire. I bought some spare tubes in Bangkok, but I have now used the last of them. I have lots of patches but still no glue, so it is with some dismay that I feel my rear tire deflate again after just thirty miles this morning. The good news is that there is a service station within sight of where I break down, so I carry Pegasus down the road and lean him against the wall of an abandoned restaurant next door. Three of the service station staff instantly surround me. They seem in dire need of the diversion I present. Sitting in an empty station on a highway in the middle of nowhere must get dull. Perhaps they can help?

I flip Pegasus upside down so the seat and handlebars are resting on the ground, take off the tire, pull out the damaged tube, and show them the patches. Then I signal that I need some glue to stick them in place. One of the guys runs to the office and comes back with a tube of Super Glue. I shake my head and point to the rubber. An excited conversation follows among the three men. Eventually one of them indicates with both hands that I should wait there, as if I could go anywhere. He jumps into a rusty car sporting four mismatched wheels and speeds off up the road.

I wait. Drink some tea. Eat some Turkish delight. Have some more tea. Wait. Three-quarters of an hour later, the car comes careering back down the road, braking at the last minute and swerving sharply to make the turn into the station. The guy jumps out with a big tub of some blue sticky substance. He is ecstatic. This *will* work! he informs me enthusiastically, head bobbing and both thumbs up.

I'm willing to try anything at this point. The patch goes on, the glue dries, and it seems to be holding well. I inflate the tube. It's still holding. I put the wheel back on the bike, thank the guys, pay the guys, and pedal away.

Blue Turkish goo is *the* glue. Who knew?

NOVEMBER 15, 2012

Two more punctures today, and I still haven't found a bike shop. The old tubes are now a mosaic of patches. The roads are very rough, which is hard on the bum and even harder on the tires. To make matters worse, my right pedal keeps popping off. Even when it stays in place, it makes a terrible clicking noise because the thread is worn, so I guess I'll need to change the whole crank. One spoke on the rear wheel has broken, and the gears are jumping again. Pegasus is tired. He needs an overhaul and a vacation.

NOVEMBER 16, 2012

In the evening I roll into a little gem of a coastal town called Ayvacık and find a lovely wood-and-stone *pensione* right on the waterfront. The sky is aflame with vibrant slashes of gold and crimson as I sit on a bench to watch the sun set over the water. Half of the exhaustion I feel on the road is mental, I remind myself, so I let my mind rest and meditate. As long as the mind stays strong, the body will follow. At this point in the cycle, it's all about keeping my head in a good place and staving off mental fatigue. I believe half the outcome of any challenge depends on state of mind. If I maintain a sense of humor about the difficult moments and always keep the end at the forefront of my thoughts, I know I will stand a better chance of emerging triumphant.

One of my coping mechanisms for dealing with pain or the stress of a particularly difficult situation is simply to laugh, as I did when suffering with diarrhea in India and after the recent dog chase. Humor is one of the best ways of getting through pain without letting it truly hurt you. Pain is an inevitable part of life, but it marks some more than others. Some people wear their pain like a layer of makeup. You can read it in every line, look, and gesture, the undercurrent of sadness like a memory connected to a song, or the lingering scent of perfume on a pillowcase. What a beautiful face it is that is unmarked; a person who has been touched by pain, yet upon whom pain has left no impression.

A genial old gentleman sits on the bench beside me. He reminds me of my uncle; with rosy cheeks and a white beard, he has aged with a natural smile etched on all his features. He looks perfectly content with himself and the world. From time to time, he strokes his moustache, smiling, his eyes far away. I wonder what memories are playing behind them. His face and eyes are so animated that I imagine he is engaged in conversation with an invisible person. I'm certain he knows a thing or two about happiness, about how to find moments of beauty and stay inside them.

NOVEMBER 18, 2012

Çanakkale is the closest city to the ancient site of Troy. The giant wooden horse from the Hollywood blockbuster stands on the beach, like a clapboard Titan guarding the coast. I'm staying the night with Tolga, a local photographer and historian with an encyclopedic knowledge of ancient history. A Turkish woman I knew from my days in Uganda contacted her friends throughout the country when she heard I would be cycling through here. Tolga is one of those friends. I like him instantly. He's short, round, and balding, with dark, dreamy eyes and a playful smile. The walls of his little apartment are covered in maps, timelines, antediluvian symbols—and his five-year-old daughter's crayon graffiti.

Like most human encyclopedias, Tolga is so full of facts and data that once the conversation starts, his stream of information flows endlessly. He fetches beers and a bottle of raki, a popular Turkish drink similar to the Italian grappa, with the flavor of aniseed. We chat, or rather he talks and I listen, into the early hours of the morning. The conversation is too interesting to contemplate sleep.

NOVEMBER 19, 2012

While grateful for Tolga's hospitality, I soon regret our late night. I should have gone to bed much earlier. Today I have been cycling protracted uphills, punctuated by a few short downhills. My muscles are tired. I am tired. Progress is slow, but at least there are no punctures, rain, or angry dogs

NOVEMBER 21, 2012

I thought the traffic in Naples was bad until I cycled through India. I believed then that it could not possibly get any worse. But it can *always* get worse. The traffic in Istanbul, the great historic portal that straddles Europe and Asia, defines a whole new level of vehicular insanity. It may be the most chaotic city I have passed through to date. I soon understand why nobody else is on a bike.

Getting from the east of the city to the west means crossing the Bosporus, and there are only two bridges, both of which are highways. If you cycle on a highway in Istanbul and live to tell the tale, you may also come out of the experience having found religion. Even the staunchest atheist will pray for life and limb when trying to navigate between the snarling dogs and the frenetic traffic. It is a toss-up which is the more dangerous; both seem intent on putting the unsuspecting cyclist in the hospital.

I reach the southwestern marina just as the sun is going

down. Another Facebook friend has offered me a bed for the night, and his family have prepared a feast in my honor. The dishes keep flowing. I recognize a few, such as a moussaka, but most of the others are new to me. I eat and eat until I think I can eat no more. Then it is time for dessert: ice cream, tea, and Turkish delight. They seem determined to keep feeding me all night, until I insist I must get an early start in the morning and head off to bed.

NOVEMBER 23, 2012

Close to the Greek border, I suffer yet another flat tire. At least this time I have some spare tubes after finding a small bike shop during my perilous trip across Istanbul. The full overhaul and a new pair of tires will have to wait. The two Turkish border guards are charming, and the three of us take turns passing around our phones for selfies. They present me with a red rose and wave me out of their wonderful country with great fanfare.

I have loved Turkey, the people, and the food. I will definitely return in the future.

A LONG WAY HOME

The Greek border official behind the window seems extremely pleased to welcome me. I was born in the little town of Rafina on the periphery of Athens, and apparently this makes me an honorary countrywoman. He wants to know what I'm doing on a bike and where I'm heading. This kicks off a long conversation about the ride and an invitation to coffee, since he is about to go for his lunch break.

It is the first decent espresso I have drunk in a very long time, and such a pleasure that I have two. Before long I am very glad I did. The Greek terrain is extremely mountainous, with long, gradual climbs that make pedaling both arduous and tedious. The uphills and descents are constant, one blending into another. Time passes and does not pass. I fade from my surroundings and withdraw into my head.

Bored with the music on my playlists after four months

with the same tunes, I now prefer to cycle in silence when I'm not listening to an audiobook. (The last book I listened to—Chuck Palahniuk's *Haunted*—was so macabre and disturbing that the day went by in a flash.) People often ask what I think about on the bike each day. I can get lost in my own head for hours, but more often than not it is less a constant stream of subconscious thought than a complete cessation of any thoughts at all. The ride becomes a kind of meditation, a time of complete stillness.

After another puncture on the road to Xanthi, my lever tool breaks as I try to change the tube. I end up walking six miles into the city, followed for the last stretch by a pack of barking dogs. A busty woman comes tearing out of a nearby farmhouse, shouting and wielding a thick stick, which she crashes down on the rump of one of the mutts. It lets out a lusty squeal and backs away. The others pause uncertainly. The woman continues yelling and waving her stick while I beat a grateful retreat.

By the time I arrive in Xanthi, I'm so shattered that I don't even bother eating. I just want to sleep. Fatigue is weighing down my limbs. My mind is tired, and my body feels like a rock. Getting up in the morning is becoming a laborious ritual that involves talking myself out of bed and onto the bike. *Come on, lazy bum, you know the drill,* I tell myself every day. *It'll be fine once you start pedaling. You won't get home unless you cycle there. So get moving.*

If all goes well, I should be home within a month. A lot can happen in a month.

NOVEMBER 24, 2012

It took an hour to change the tube this morning, using the tip of a knife as a makeshift lever. I have no grip left in my hands—my thumb and forefinger can barely hold a fork to eat—so I needed a lever to get the tire off and back on the rim. I wonder whether I'm setting some kind of Guinness World Record for the most punctures suffered on one journey. Pegasus has already had twenty-six. At least there are some good tailwinds today, and I manage to cover the 140 miles into Thessaloniki without further interruption.

Some kind of fair is going on in the city. All the hotels and hostels are full, so I spend a couple of hours trying to find a bed for the night. When you're tired, spending valuable time looking for a place to stay instead of sleeping is enough to make you lose it and break into a tearful stomping fit. I am desperate. I am exhausted. As if that is not enough, I have also started my period.

The red neon vacancy sign over a sex shop, illuminated by a pink light above the entrance, is all the invitation I need. I don't care where I sleep, as long as it has a bed—and some peace and quiet. I need a long sleep tonight, but the loud moans and squeals from next door prevent that. Seriously, any woman that loud has to be faking it.

I wake up after a rough night to find the rear tire deflated once again. My mood instantly follows suit. Poor Pegasus is feeling the wear and tear of the road. He is in urgent need of that long-promised overhaul, so I find a large bike shop and ask the mechanic to fit new tires, chain, pedals, and cranks. With that done, we should be ready for the final twenty-six hundred miles to the finish line.

The road west toward Ioannina winds over a long mountain pass—more than sixty miles uphill. The towns dotting the valley below gradually become tiny specks, then disappear altogether. The hours tick by in peaceful silence, punctuated only by the chirping of birds and crickets and the rhythm of my own breathing. Thick white clouds hang low over the mountains, and as I near the top of the climb, I can see them spread across the peaks below me like a soft blanket of snow. On the summit there is nothing but blue sky above and white clouds below. It is a strange sensation—like climbing into the sky and another world. I get a strong sense of déjà vu, like I have been here before.

When I was a child, I had a number of recurring dreams. Most nights I dreamed of monsters chasing me. No matter how hard I tried to run, I couldn't escape; my legs felt slow and heavy, as if I were running through mud. The monsters would close in, and I would sometimes awake just as I felt the hot breath of their massive jaws on my back. At other times they would catch me, and I would feel myself dying just as I woke up. Eventually I learned how to pull myself out of the dream and wake up just before they reached me. Waking hours, on the other hand, were filled with monsters I couldn't escape.

One recurring dream was different, and because of its nature and frequency, it has remained firmly planted in my memory. In the initial dream I was a small girl of five, walking with my father, my tiny hand enveloped by his large one. "I want to show you something," he said, leading me down a series of dark alleyways in a poor slum in one of the developing countries where we lived, possibly the Philippines or Sri Lanka. Turning down one of the dusty streets, we came to a dead end where there was a long cement staircase, leading somewhere out of sight. We climbed the steps together, my hand still clasping his, my eyes never quite able to see where the stairs were leading. Then without me really understanding how, the stairs ended, and all at once we were inside another world—one that was more beautiful than anywhere I had ever seen. Flowers of every color stretched into infinity. The air was fresh and scented with their perfume. The sky was such a deep shade of blue that it was almost purple. Everything was bathed in a golden light, though there was no visible sun. My senses tingled with smells, colors, and sensations I had never experienced before. I let go of my father's hand and ran squealing through the lush fields in a state of total bliss. Completely happy, completely free. I forgot the world below where we lived. This was where I wanted to stay forever.

In the subsequent dreams my father was absent, and I

never managed to enter that magical world again. Alone, I would search for the mysterious stairway, racing desperately through streets that led nowhere, blocked by people, traffic, and obstacles. Sometimes I would be chased by an unnamed, unseen threat; at other times I was in a war zone, dodging bombs and bullets. Sweaty, hungry, and tired, I would never give up the search. I had to find those stairs and get back to that place, return to the hidden Shangri-La before the stairway disappeared from my dreams forever. Occasionally I would find the steps, but I never managed to climb to the top and see that beautiful place again.

Now, without even looking for it, here I am! This is the place! That same feeling of total elation and happiness overwhelms me. I want to cry and laugh at the same time. After all those years searching for it, deep down I have always known the way back, but it was buried under suffering and sorrow and struggles. Today I have stumbled on it by accident, and now I understand. I don't need a staircase to reach this place of complete bliss. I can find it anywhere, at any time.

It reminds me of something Joseph Campbell wrote: "Find a place inside where there's joy, and the joy will burn out the pain."

Today I have found that place.

NOVEMBER 27, 2012

I ride across the Albanian border just before it shuts at eight p.m. The countryside is majestic, with the terrain largely uninhabited and very mountainous. There is nothing but wilderness save for a few small towns and one or two cities sparsely scattered across the country.

Winter is setting in, the days are short now, and night closes over me before I can reach Sarandë, even though it's only twelve miles from the border. Somewhere along the road I pull up short. Hundreds of glowing eyes are staring out from the darkness, illuminated by my headlight. It's creepy. The New Zealand horror film *Black Sheep* comes to mind. I slowly roll through the herd of sheep as their eyes silently follow my back.

Even with my bright headlight, the blackness is nearly impenetrable. But there are stars—a glorious, infinite firmament of stars. The giant globes of fiery gas that could consume our planet look like tiny glittering specks, so small and distant. I can't help thinking that we, with our inflated sense of our own importance, are just infinitesimal particles in a giant cosmos, and that the things that occupy our daily lives are meaningless when seen through the lens of eternity. We're nothing but minute, insignificant organisms who believe we're the center of the universe. How ridiculous is the human race? How ridiculous am I? We're insignificant. Cycling around the world, I'm insignificant. The universe was here before, and it will continue long after my brief spell of consciousness.

And yet perhaps, on a subconscious level, this was one of the many reasons I set off to cycle around the world. To celebrate the unlikelihood of this existence. To leave my footprint in the cement, like a caveman leaving his inscription on the wall of a cave. Maybe creating a legacy is all any of us are really after; why people have children, write books, compose music, paint pictures: so they can leave behind something that says, *Against all the odds, I was here. For one brief moment in time, I existed.*

Nothing comes easy today, starting with the toughest, longest, and steepest mountain I've encountered so far, heading out of the small coastal town of Kondraq. It's such hard going and the bike feels so heavy that I have to dismount and walk part of the way up. Nearing the summit, in the middle of a series of switchbacks, I am buffeted by strong winds, rain, and fog. I stop in the restaurant at the top to get dry and warm. I can hear the wind howling outside and can see the clouds swirling thickly by. It takes a couple of hours and several plates of food to work up the courage to head back out into the elements.

The descent is even more harrowing than the ascent. I can see no more than a few yards in front of me, and mighty gusts of wind shake Pegasus from side to side. There are no guard rails, and my imagination starts working overtime as I picture flying over the edge. The rain stings, whipped up by a wind that pummels me so hard, even pedaling is out of the question for several long stretches. As a result, coming down the mountain takes almost as long as going up.

Finally back on flat roads, getting to the city of Vlorë is still a mission. I struggle for every mile into a headwind, as the rain continues to come down relentlessly. I reach the city limits and decide I am just too wet and drained of willpower to carry on. I've cycled only seventy-five miles today—just over half my normal distance.

One nice surprise awaits me, though. Nicola, who spent a week with me in India, has caught the ferry over from Italy with another friend, Angela. Seeing a couple of friendly faces is a rare pleasure. We share a twenty-five-dollar room for three in a cheap hotel, eat a giant dinner of steak and fries, and drink beer. While I generally enjoy being alone on the road, I have to admit I've also missed the human company. Too much of anything is too much, even solitude.

NOVEMBER 29, 2012

"You're almost there!" says Nicola as he and Angela hug me goodbye after a last lunch together not far from the Albania/Montenegro border. "People are starting to get excited now you're almost back in Italy. We're gonna have a huge party to welcome you back. Just sixteen hundred to go. Piece of cake!"

He's right. After sixteen thousand miles, sixteen hundred doesn't sound too bad. If I can keep up my average of 125 a day, I should be home in time for Christmas. My sister Lily is coming to spend the holidays with me and Antonio. I know I'll eat and eat as if every piece of food has a short expiration date.

NOVEMBER 30, 2012

I am held up at the border for two hours in a hailstorm. The bad weather then follows me into Montenegro, where I stop early for the second time in three days to get clean and dry. Checking into a cheap hotel in Podgorica, I log on to the Internet and receive some terrible news. My friend Jesse, who put me up in Brisbane, was hit by a truck on the Gold Coast, on the very same road that we had pedaled together a couple of months back. I message his wife, Maria, and she replies that Jesse is still in hospital, and has just come out of a coma.

"It's such an irony," Maria writes. "Here you cycle around the world through crazy countries like India and nothing happens to you, while he cycles the same road to work every day, and this happens."

I agree to such an extent that I almost feel guilty for having made it nearly the whole way around the globe unscathed. I sit on the hotel bed, munching a packet of peanuts, rain still pelting against the window, and think about how the world is full of irony. There are the basic, constant laws of the universe, on which everything depends, and which our lives follow with comfortable predictability. We like to think we have some semblance of control over our lives or that some greater power has control over them. That we can make sense of whatever happens to us. That there is some greater purpose to it all, a reason for all the suffering and pain, something to justify the imbalances we see every day in the world around us. We want to feel safe, secure against every eventuality, so we construct worlds of illusion into which we bury our heads like the proverbial ostrich.

But then something completely random, something for which we are totally unprepared, is thrown into the mix, and we suddenly realize that, for all its laws, for all its order, the universe is full of chaos, and all our carefully laid plans are useless. This never hit home harder for me than the day Hendri died. It was a painful reminder that the only sure thing in life is that nothing lasts, including life itself. Among all our many uncertainties, that is the one irrevocable certainty.

You know that film *The Bucket List*, about two guys who are diagnosed with terminal cancer and decide to tick off a list of all their greatest wishes and desires? They end up doing everything they previously feared because they know they are dying, so what's the worst that could happen? The truth is, from the day we are born, time starts counting down toward that one inevitability. All we ever have is time. Yet even time is an illusion. All that really exists is the eternal present. We can only ever live right now, in this day, this hour, this minute.

Hendri called it "living the best day ever." It was the guiding philosophy by which he lived his life. Yesterday is always in the past; it no longer exists. Tomorrow has not yet happened, so it does not exist either. Today is the only day we will ever live, and that makes it the best day ever. The sooner we realize this, the sooner we can stop holding on so tightly to what we think we have, stop hoarding in preparation for an elusive future, and start going about the business of living in the present. Because all that exists is now. This moment. This day.

DECEMBER 5, 2012

I am physically and mentally exhausted. I have crossed many mountains, but the last few have seemed endless. On the final steep climb in Slovenia, just a few miles from the Italian border, I have a mental breakdown. Unable to pedal any farther, I burst into tears on the phone to Antonio, muttering, "I can't, I can't, I can't."

He is concerned. This is the first time he has ever heard me use the word "can't," so he knows it must be serious. "Ju, just stop for today. Turn around, go back down the hill, and find a place to rest."

The words "stop" and "go back" work like vinegar on a wound. Anything but that. Going back has never been an option. In the words of Dr. Livingstone, "I will go anywhere, provided it be forward."

Stop being such a baby, I scold myself. *There's nobody to get you home but yourself, and the only way to get home is to move. So move!*

I walk my bike up the last stretch of the climb, remount near the top, and pedal victoriously across the border and into Italy. A couple of cyclists from the Salvaiciclisti, or "Save the Cyclists," a group that campaigns for rights on the road, have been following my journey online and are waiting to escort me into Trieste. I am back in Italia! As soon as we hit the city center, I insist on stopping at a bar for a good coffee. Ah, espresso—how I have missed you! It is not Neapolitan coffee, but it is pretty good all the same.

My two companions are putting me up for the night, but first we have dinner with more cyclists from Salvaiciclisti, and I tell them all about my travels. They warn me that the temperature is about to drop dramatically and snow is expected within the next couple of days. Having lived in tropical climates most of my life, my body does not adapt well to extreme cold. Couple that with not having adequate clothing or equipment for anything below forty degrees Fahrenheit, and the forecast is grim. I can only hope that by some miracle I will clear northern Italy before the snow starts to fall.

DECEMBER 8, 2012

Two years ago today, I was sitting on the sofa, scrolling through my Facebook news feed, when I saw the news of Hendri's death. I was in shock for the first couple of days, unable to believe that it was real. When at last it sank in that I would never see him alive again, my world went dark. I couldn't imagine living in a world without him.

I believe that some people enter our lives for a reason. They may not stay long, but they have a lasting effect. Hendri was such a person for me. Today I'm just a couple of weeks away from finishing a world circumnavigation by bicycle, a journey I never would have thought possible two years ago. The irony is not lost on me. If Hendri had not died, I never would have done something this extreme. I never would have known I could cycle any distance at all, let alone around the world. His death was the catalyst that launched my life in a different direction. That seeded a new passion. That awoke a hunger for new experiences, discovery, and self-realization.

Yet I would press rewind, give up everything I have seen and done and experienced, just to see him once more, to have one more conversation with him. I tried to hold on to his memory, tried to keep him alive for as long as I could. I thought that if I didn't accept his death, it wouldn't exist. This cycle ride has been as much an inward journey as a physical one, a symbolic act of release, of letting him go, of realizing that life keeps moving forward and so must I.

The most beautiful things in life are fleeting. That is part of their beauty. To have something go on and on forever would dilute its potency. I loved Hendri. The moments we shared were beautiful and always will be. The passing of time can never change that. But the cycle of life goes on; and with death, something new is born.

On this day last year I cried, but I am not crying today. In fact, I no longer cry when I think of him. When his face appears in my mind, he is smiling. I whisper the words he wrote in one of his last blogs like a prayer:

Thank you for the flat rock I sleep on.
Thank you for the peace I feel.
Thank you for the chance to live my dreams.

THE IMPOSSIBLE DREAM

The snow has arrived, as predicted. Light flakes were falling as I wheeled up to a *pensione* in Olmi last night, and I awake to a steady snowfall. The countryside is already covered with a powdery white blanket. The flakes keep coming down, soaking through my gloves and shoes. The sun eventually breaks through the fog, but it makes little difference. I am wearing three pairs of socks and two pairs of gloves, but somehow the wet and cold still penetrate.

When the sun shines, the cold is just about tolerable. But daylight hours are short and getting shorter. I watch each sunset with dread. In the darkness, the black ice on the roads is treacherous, the freezing temperatures unbearable. I am doing everything I can just to keep my core warm. I stop at a bar after dark to try to get some feeling back into my hands and feet. Remembering how well the bourbon worked in New Zealand, I order a shot of whiskey from the bartender.

"Whiskey?" he repeats, not sure he has heard me correctly.

"*Sì. Whiskey. Fa freddo.*" It's cold.

He smiles and shrugs, pulls out a tumbler, and fills it to the top with the equivalent of at least three shots. I drain it in one go.

"*Ancora?*" Another? There is admiration in his voice.

Why the hell not? At least I will be cycling happy and hopefully numb. He tops up the glass.

"Cheers." I raise my glass to him and down it in one again. A delicious heat spreads through my chest.

The bartender is so impressed that he charges me just two euros for my shots and waves me off. My hands and feet are still ice cold, but for the first time since the snow started falling, I cycle with some semblance of warmth in my core.

DECEMBER 11, 2012

I have reached the point of total exhaustion. My body is ready to quit. I could collapse right now if I let myself. The temperature has dropped to sixteen degrees Fahrenheit; the bitter cold drains the little energy I have left. I'm eating every couple of hours just to stay warm. My face is raw with wind-burn, my lips cracked and dry. Blood is running from my nose, and I cannot stop coughing. My hands are swollen and blistered from the cold. My feet no longer ache, but only because I can't feel them. What I can feel is a dull pain deep within my bones traveling from my ankles up to my knees.

Instead of keeping to my usual schedule—stopping once for food after sixty miles—I am forced to take more frequent breaks to warm up and get the blood circulating through my limbs again. I stop at bars along the road, ordering double hot chocolates and stuffing down whatever food they have on offer: panini, *cornetti* with Nutella, pastries, and pies. It's like feeding a dying furnace. I sidle up against the heaters, body trembling, lips blue.

I am still on track to finish in 150 days, but all these stops are consuming valuable time.

My feet are not a pretty sight when I pull off my shoes at the end of the day. Two of my toes are black; the rest are a deep, raw red, covered in painful chilblains, with dead yellow toenails . Tomorrow they will refreeze, and the blisters will grow. If I can just get farther south, where it is warmer, I am hoping the damage will not be permanent.

Bob Marley reportedly said, "You never know how strong you are until being strong is your only choice." I have reached the point where I have nothing left in me. My body should be giving up. Even my willpower has gone. At this level of mental and physical exhaustion, the slightest hill feels like a mountain, the gentlest gust a hurricane. There are only about nine hundred miles left, but it might as well be nine thousand. Every day feels like a week, every hour a day. I know it's almost over, but today it seems as if it will never end. Every tiny setback mushrooms out of all proportion, but the idea of curling into a tearful ball and sucking my thumb makes me crack a smile. Perhaps the only thing keeping me going now is sheer dumb stubborn tenacity. I never seem to run out of *that*.

Many people have written to compliment me on my strength throughout this endeavor. But I am not strong. I am the furthest thing from strong. I have suffered deep pain. I have lost everything I had and the people I loved most. There have been days when death seemed like a tempting gift and continuing to live the most difficult thing in the world. But I have kept on going because I am stubborn. When the pain becomes too much to bear, when I am too tired to carry on, my tenacity and pride force me onward. Giving up completely would be even harder, because I could never live with myself if I did.

DECEMBER 14, 2012

I should reach Ancona, on the east coast of Italy, within the next day or two, and the temperature will rise with every mile south from there. The sun will be a game changer for me, physically and mentally. I am back on my own SIM card and have ready access to wi-fi. Reading people's messages of support on Facebook is a great boost to my morale.

Since I am online more often now, bits and pieces of news from the real world start to reach me on the road. There has been a terrible tragedy in the States today. A young guy went into a primary school and shot twenty children and six teachers. Everybody is screaming about the need for more gun control, and while I agree that would be a good thing, I cannot help thinking that guns are not the problem. Human nature is the problem.

Cycling around the world has helped me to see our planet through new eyes, to challenge the preconceptions I held about myself, society, and other individuals. I have suffered from a feeling of disconnection from other people for many years, never able to shake the sense that I am different and don't belong, thereby isolating myself from what is essentially the human experience. I imagine it is a similar feeling of isolation, taken to an extreme degree, that prompts a young man to walk into a primary school and start shooting.

The more people I have met from different backgrounds and cultures, and the more I have listened to them speak about the things that are important to them, the more I have realized that while we may differ in some of the details, we are all fundamentally connected. We are all here, just trying to figure it out, trying to find a purpose, in pursuit of happiness. Yet instead of focusing on our commonalities, we look at our differences. We segregate, we judge, we assume. We live in a world of "us and them." We are riddled with prejudices and moral superiority, separated by religion, race, belief, color, social status, wealth, poverty.

I have been listening to a lot of Charles Bukowski over the last week. It was probably his dark, absurdist understanding of human nature that drove him to the bottle, but his dysfunctional genius was pretty spot on a lot of the time. "We're all going to die, all of us," he says through my earphones. "What a circus! That alone should make us love each other, but it doesn't. We are terrorized and flattened by trivialities. We are eaten up by nothing."

The headwinds and rain from Cerignola to Specchia are soul destroying. I made good progress down the southeast coast, pushed by a tailwind the whole way. The road was flat, and the temperature increased a little every day. But now I have turned inland, heading toward the west coast and Naples, the winds are against me once more. I keep telling myself, *Almost home now. You can endure just a little more misery.* You can endure anything when there is a foreseeable end.

Antonio calls to tell me a massive welcome party is being organized in Naples for my return. I know he is trying to keep that finish line at the forefront of my thoughts. He can hear I'm fading every time he calls. As tired as I am, I can only guess how exhausted he must be. I know he has slept less than I have over the last five months, setting his alarm at odd hours of the night to check my progress on the tracker and make sure I'm still moving forward. Through all the ups and downs of this adventure, he has been my one, utterly dependable rock. I could not have done it without his support. This journey has not been mine alone; he has shared each and every moment with me. That finish line cannot come soon enough for both of us.

The support I have received throughout Italy has made this last stretch to the end a little easier to bear. Hotels have put me up for free all along the route home. Restaurants have offered free meals. It may sound silly, but having a good bed for the night and good food to eat right now is making the difference between whether I make it back in time for Christmas or not.

DECEMBER 20, 2012

I am just under 250 miles from the finish line, but it feels like five thousand. Every day it is a struggle just to keep pedaling. The moment I stop, all I can think of is collapsing somewhere and sleeping. It is hard to believe that the journey is almost at an end. Some days it feels as if it will never end. Even my dreams are full of planning routes and pedaling . . . endlessly. Pegasus is tired, too. He has endured twenty-nine punctures, eight broken spoke nipples, two broken derailleurs, and four tire changes. I have pedaled over six big mountains, across one desert, and through a cyclone. I have cycled with diarrhea, high fevers, and a chest infection. I have been attacked by countless dogs, magpies, and horseflies. Pegasus and I have conquered every challenge, achieved things I never would have thought possible a year ago. I should feel invincible, but I just feel old.

I often wondered whether I had what it takes to see this endeavor through to the end. I guess I have my answer and have proved my point. We can do things that are greater than ourselves. If you believe nothing exists beyond a certain boundary, then you will never test the veracity of that belief and you will never discover new possibilities. If I had waited to achieve a higher level of fitness, to hone my cycling technique and mechanical know-how, to ensure the best weather conditions, to assemble a full support team, to secure a sponsor and more funding, I never would have left. Many people postpone making their dreams a reality to wait for the perfect time. There's no such thing. The perfect time is right now.

The word "extraordinary" keeps popping up on Facebook as people share posts about my journey. Funny . . . it was "crazy" when I set out. Maybe there are truly extraordinary people out there, but I'm not one of them. The most extraordinary acts are accomplished by ordinary people doing something a little extra and stepping outside their personal comfort zone. That little extra means something different for each individual.

Who am I? Nobody important, nobody special, nobody especially talented or athletic. I would never have known that I could cycle at all, much less cycle around the world, had I not gotten on a bike and tried. I often wonder just how much human potential lies unrealized and untapped, how much we are limited by our own fears as well as by social, cultural, religious, and self-imposed limitations. If we can break through those, how far might we go as individuals, as a species?

DECEMBER 22, 2012

The weather forecast has predicted rain. As I dress for my last ride, the morning sky is spotted with gray clouds, just as it was on the day I set off. A group of cyclists have gathered at the bar across the street, waiting for me to come down. Then the Harley motorcade of leather-clad old-timers pulls up in a clamor of horns and sirens. "Oh Happy Day" blasts from speakers attached to their gleaming motorbikes. At eight-thirty a.m. in this quiet residential neighborhood in Cardito, all the commotion seems incongruous if not slightly ludicrous.

I watch them uneasily through the beaded balcony curtain and half-contemplate slipping out through the back door and riding home quietly, back to my own apartment.

"*Sei pronta?*"—Are you ready?—Antonio's mother asks me, laughing at the cornered look on my face, much as she laughed at the brown-black water in her tub after I bathed in it. I rode into Cardito yesterday evening and stayed the night at the home of Antonio's family. I cringed and apologized when the little group of waiting friends, his parents, and his brother embraced me. I stank so badly that even my Jack Russell, Mela, shrank from me.

Today I am clean, smelling of peach and vanilla bath gel, my cycling clothes freshly laundered. Today is my victory celebration, and all the pandemonium downstairs is for me. The crowd is steadily growing. At nine a.m. it's time to face the music. Literally. "Jingle Bells" is now crackling from the motorbike speakers. Surreal, all of it. I pull on my jacket, torn at the left sleeve from one of many falls, snatch up my helmet and gloves, and head downstairs.

"She's coming!" someone calls as I cross the street, feeling all eyes turn toward me.

I dislike crowds, and I hate being stared at, so I keep my eyes fixed on the pavement till I reach Antonio. His voice has been the only constant throughout the ever-changing scenery and terrain, towns and cities, mountains, wilderness and deserts, food, currencies, and cultures. I can scarcely believe he has been half a world away for most of the last five months; rather, he seems to have been just next door. Seeing him again at the end of the road is like hugging a security blanket I have carried with me everywhere.

"Ready?" he asks. He is probably even more relieved than I am that it is finally almost over.

Cardito's mayor and the director of culture and sport come over to shake my hand, kiss me on the cheeks, and present me with a plaque.

COMUNE DI CARDITO

To Juliana Buhring,

Linked from the heart to our land, leaving in Cardito

the last imprint of her epic undertaking as the

first woman to circumnavigate the globe,

cycling in defense of Children's Rights.

Thank you.

I thank them in return and walk over to the waiting cyclists, shaking their hands. "*Ciao. Buongiorno.*"

"She has a weird accent," one of them says. "Where's she from?"

"America," someone else says.

"No, I heard she was born in Greece."

I smile. I'm from nowhere and from everywhere. I can hear Hendri's voice in my head:

Perhaps we are merely the transition; we have "lost" our old self the way a snake sheds its old skin. We are not strangers from life, we have lived as fully as any, and we are not outsiders because of the same reason. We are not lost because, as you say, we have merely been going for a walk. So who are we? . . . My favorite question.

Like a work in progress, my identity continues to grow and change with every new piece of culture, experience, and idea I absorb. My lack of attachment to any particular culture, location, or possession has given me the freedom to question and explore outside the usual constraints of familial, religious, or social expectations. I can be at home no matter where I am in the world. Instead of asking where I'm from, perhaps a better question would be, Where am I going?

Today I am going to the Piazza del Plebiscito and the finish line of the world cycle. Is it really over? "One last ride, Pegasus," I whisper, clinging to my bicycle as if he were an anchor in a storm of noise, shouting, horns, and music. I

have been alone on the road for so long that being surrounded by so many people is making me nervous. I am glad
when the formalities are over and I can finally get back on
my bike and ride, as I have done every day for the last five
months. I clip in and kick off.

Back in my element, the noises around me fade. Head
down, hunched over the bike frame, I pedal on autopilot, a
slice away from reality, all thoughts temporarily out of reach.
I forget the world, and a stillness spreads inside me. I am a
lone satellite orbiting the Earth. The road embodies something abstract and immaterial. Eternity.

EPILOGUE

I often find myself staring out of my apartment window in Naples, into the horizon, at the sky. I cannot tell you how long I have stood there. It is a bit like sleepwalking—not really here, not really awake. I pedaled 18,063 miles in 144 days, across 19 countries and 4 continents, averaging over 125 miles each day. I also set the first woman's record for fastest circumnavigation of the world by bicycle with a total time of 152 days.

What is there for me to do now?

Everyone wants to know what the journey was like. But how can I explain the power, the rush of being alive, of feeling connected to everything, of simply "being"? Pedaling over the finish line was anticlimactic in comparison. I felt a kind of deflation, a withdrawal after the high I had been riding on for five months. I still miss being on the open road, heading into the wind and the unknown. All I can think about is achieving that high once more.

Why do adventurers and adrenaline junkies do the crazy things they do? Are they a particular breed? Or do they just wake up one morning and say, *What if I try this one thing?* and before they know it, that one thing leads to another and another? Perhaps chasing that elusive high becomes their drug, so they will do anything, even risk death, to experience it again.

I think many of them, including Hendri, subconsciously yearn for death as a kind of release from the disappointment and mediocrity they find most of human existence to be. Chasing the high becomes ever more difficult, and the depressive inertia of the in-between times increasingly unbearable, so they run at things, seek out risk, look for any way to rise into the air.

On his way back from a solo expedition to the Congo, a journey that deeply affected him and his view of life, Hendri wrote:

There are few times in my life I feel as lost and lonely as when I return from a long mission. When you realize that no matter what you have been through, that no matter how much you might have sacrificed or learned, the world does not care. The world functions perfectly fine superficially.

You feel the sadness creeping in when you hear people around you complain about a bad day and you know that in a month or two their simple worries will be yours again. In the weeks or months that it takes to readjust, you are left to wonder how what seemed so significant on your journey can now seem so everyday.

In the first few weeks following my return home, I did not have a whole lot to say. In fact, I had trouble talking at all and found it difficult to find commonalities on which to build conversations or bonds with people on any level. I also didn't realize just how mentally and physically exhausted I was. I had promised myself I would stay fit and keep cycling when I got home. My spirit was willing; my flesh, not so much. I was unable to will my body to get on that bike again. Perhaps memories of the suffering I had endured got in the way.

But the most difficult part of all has been trying to reacclimatize to "normalcy." Some days I am nervous and snappy from inaction; others I am reluctant to open the curtains and just want to stay under a blanket. I go out of my way to socialize with friends and immerse myself in human contact. And I think that getting back on the bike will do me good, when I feel I can manage it. My body needs some physical stimulation before I start punching walls.

I recently heard from another world cyclist, Mike Hall, who invited me to enter the first ever unsupported cycle race across Europe—from London to Istanbul. I felt my pulse quickening at the thought of a fresh adventure. Perhaps the best way to recover from the last challenge is to start planning a new one.

I have no money. I have not been on a bike for four

months. The race isn't far off. I will be the only female competitor. I have never entered a bike race before, let alone one against a bunch of men. As usual, my friends say I'm crazy. Their advice is to rest for at least a year. Antonio warns me that riding around the world and racing are two very different things: "You're not a racer. Maybe it's too soon to start planning another adventure."

But you know what happens when I'm told I cannot or should not do something. That little voice in my head starts counting down . . .*

---

* Juliana was the only woman to race the inaugural Transcontinental Race from London to Istanbul in 2013. She cycled 3,400 kilometers in 12 days, finishing in ninth place overall. The following year she was the first female finisher—and tied fourth overall—in the Trans Am Bike Race, riding 7,137 kilometers in 20 days and 23 hours. Having cycled seriously for the first time in 2011, at the age of thirty, she is now considered one of the strongest female ultra-endurance cyclists in the world. Her around-the-world record remains unbroken at the time of writing.

ACKNOWLEDGMENTS

Antonio Zullo has been the person in my corner from the beginning, and as such, I must begin by thanking him. Antonio, this book is only a small piece of a much bigger story that only you and I will ever fully know or understand and maybe it is better that way. Thank you for believing in me when no one else did, for bringing out the best in me and helping me to realize my full potential as an individual. Know that you have been, and forever will be, an important part of my existence.

To my manager, Steven Rosen, thank you for believing that this story should be told enough to make this book happen, for sticking around during the times when I was difficult to deal with, for your professional tenacity, and for many acts of selflessness which eventually won me over (that and your enthusiastic overuse of the word "amazing").

Thanks to my agent Caspian Dennis for handling me, my mistakes and occasional irascibility with the calm and grace of a gentleman.

Thank you Joy Tutela for taking me around New York in the rain when you had a baby waiting at home. You are a super woman!

I am further grateful to the incredible team at W. W. Norton who shaped my scribblings into something legible and without whom this book would not exist. Thank you Alane Mason and Marie Pantojan for your guidance and patience.

It is easy to declare "I cycled around the world," but the fact is, I would never have managed it without all the individuals who contributed monetarily and morally to keep me on the road. Whether it was a thousand dollars or fifty, all gave what they could and in the end it added up to a world record. So to all my friends and supporters who believed in my mad dream and helped to make it a reality, thank you.

- Thomas Kelly (USA)
- Chris McDonald (Australia)
- David and Echo (France)
- Steven Levithan (USA)
- Mariana Buhring (France)
- Richard & Zanny Martin (Switzerland)
- Jason Scott (USA)
- Mario Schiano (Italy)
- Siobhan Stella (Ireland)
- Guido Notari (Uganda)
- Marek Hamšík (Napoli footballer)
- Peter Frouman (USA)
- Katrina Levithan (USA)

- Elio Zullo (Italy)
- Mauro Russo (Italy)
- Antonio Vitello (Italy)
- Riccardo & Angela Zullo (Italy)
- Erinn LaMattery (Japan)
- Whisper Wind James (USA)
- Jesse Martin Nolan (USA)
- Michele Auriemma & Carmen (Italy)
- Michele Gentile (Italy)
- Ilaria Martini (Italy)
- Bruce & Michelle Warren (USA)
- Marco Auriemma (Italy)
- Paolo Chan (USA)
- Kathryn Mercogliano (USA)
- Kelly Rugely (USA)
- John Mageropoulos (USA)
- Fiona McLeod (UK)
- Kai Hayes (USA)
- Stephanie Mills (UK)
- Starr Guckert (USA)
- Claire Turquin-Silhouette (France)
- Isabelle Chouar et le Gambrinus (France)
- David Hose (USA)
- Lynn Etherton (USA)
- Romolo Ponzo (Italy)
- Marco Martini (Italy)
- Gesualdo Di Prospero (Italy)
- Salvatore Alfieri (Italy)
- The Bennett family (New Zealand)

- Vincent Miller (Australia)
- The Fawkin Hawkins (Australia)
- Anthony Booths (Australia)
- Angel Smith (Australia)
- Maria Gabriella Berti (Italy)
- James Benson (USA)
- Vincenzo Fedele (Italy)
- Mark Jacobs (USA)
- Petra Laila Bartlett (USA)
- Dacil Bettinger (USA)
- Michael McMahon (Australia)
- Sean Preece (England)
- Floriana De Stefano (Italy)
- Gina M. Catena (Italy)
- Clara Comelli (Italy)
- Tommaso Fortunato (Italy)